"Walker is a lifelong student of sales and a [...] self-help preacher. He has an uncanny ability to break down any issue into its basic components, and he probes with direct questions that lead to self-discovery. His quick wit, self-deprecating style and flair for colorful language make this book impossible to put down."

—FITZHUGH KING, Senior Vice President,
Southern First Bank

"Walker has a rare personality that allows him—almost forces him—to enter uncomfortable territory and come out the other side with hilarious stories and sales insights for the rest of us. Walker made me laugh and then smile by teaching me to relax during the sales process. Whew!"

—JOHN STERLING, Founder,
Sterling Sales Company

"*Some Will. Some Won't. So What. Who's Next?* is relatable and applicable. Too often sales books are either sloppy pop-psychology or, at the other end of the spectrum, boring treatises on esoteric theory. This book is neither. Walker's stories are compelling, and his practical wisdom is immediately useful."

—PERRIN DesPORTES, Co-Founder & Partner,
Polaris Healthcare Partners

"Walker does a remarkable job breaking down the sales process. A natural storyteller and seasoned sales trainer, Walker cuts through the standard sales BS by giving readers a better understanding of prospective clients and how to effectively solve their problems."

—CHRIS SIMMONS, Founder,
Industrial Network Group and Total Industrial

"If you think succeeding in sales means you have to be slick or sleazy, Walker's alternative take will blow your mind. By following his No

BS Sales approach, you will maintain your integrity and boost your business."

—LINDSEY MCMILLION STEMANN,
LinkedIn Credibility Consultant, Speaker & Founder,
McMillion Consulting

"Trust me: This isn't a run-of-the-mill sales manual. Between Walker's candid and very funny personal stories and his well-honed sales method, *Some Will. Some Won't* is hard to put down. Once you're done, you'll be forever changed—for the better."

—DAISY MILLER, President,
Forest Lake Travel

"If you're not prepared to rethink how you communicate to everyone in your life, then this book is not for you. But, if you're willing to listen—to take time to understand what those around you are saying—then Walker will help you have more productive conversations with your spouse, kids, friends and co-workers. AND you will sell more. A lot more."

—JAMIE LYNCH, Director,
ES Integrated

"For the past 20 years, Walker has given me the advice I needed to stand up straight, stop making excuses and do the work required to grow my sales. Read this book, and you'll understand why I continue to turn to Walker."

—MATT NETTLETON, President,
Sandler DTB Training

"*Some Will. Some Won't* is the ultimate guide for quickly moving past the 'No's' and finding the 'Yes's' that will grow your business."

—ROBERT SCOTT, Vice President,
Atlantic Forklift Services

"Readable and totally relatable, *Some Will. Some Won't. So What. Who's Next?* will not only boost your sales, but it will make you a better, more authentic version of yourself."

—CATHY MONETTI, Founder,
Riggs Partners

"Walker McKay helped me uncover a personal power I didn't know I had. He taught me how to say 'No,' and that opened up a world of possibilities."

—CHRISTOPHER DECKER, CEO,
Creator Spark

"Walker's book is witty, fun and, above all, helpful. His nontraditional approach will boost your bottom line and improve your outlook."

—KEVIN SMITH, Partner,
Riggs Partners

"Walker's coaching, wit and practical advice have leveled up my own sense of confidence in establishing a deep pipeline and closing more profitable deals."

—OLLY SUMMERS, Vice President/Director of Service,
Way Engineering

"Walker's book is far from another sales manual. It's a blueprint for rethinking how you approach your entire business."

—CHRIS KING, Co-founder,
IDV, creators of SpeedTree software

"Walker gets it like so few do. Tactics, techniques, strategies and systems are all helpful. But more than anything, success in sales begins with the eight inches between your ears—how you think about selling, how you position yourself, how you play the game. All of these things are indispensable. In his book, Walker lays out a clear path to BE the person you need to be to find success."

—Chris Caldwell, Founder,
Sell As You Are

"*Some Will. Some Won't* is an articulate, creative and innovative take on the sales process. Walker's methodology has helped me connect and communicate with my clients more effectively. He transformed the sales process from a daunting task to the foundation of how I build client relationships. I can't recommend this book highly enough!"

—Vella Petrova, Senior Brand Manager,
2 Market Media

"*Some Will. Some Won't* redefines the rules of sales for today's world. Walker delivers a practical process you can use on your next prospect call, with his signature 'No BS' approach and great storytelling. This is a book you'll find yourself referring to again and again."

—Anna Roberts, Manager,
MothWorks at The Moth

"If you want to learn how to stop giving free advice, start working with your ideal clients and closing bigger deals (faster), then this is a must-read for you. From shedding old beliefs to adopting new ones and learning to tactfully implement these selling skills, *Some Will. Some Won't. So What. Who's Next?* covers it all."

—Vaughn Granger, Founder,
Liam John USA

SOME WILL.
SOME WON'T.
SO WHAT.
WHO'S NEXT?

SOME WILL.
SOME WON'T.
SO WHAT.
WHO'S NEXT?

A Blueprint for Sales Success from
the Creator of the **No BS Sales System**™

WALKER McKAY

For information about this title, contact the publisher:

Walker McKay Books
Columbia, SC
www.walkermckay.com

ISBNs:
979-8-9905048-0-6 (softcover)
979-8-9905048-1-3 (eBook)

Printed in the United States of America

Cover and Interior design: 1106 Design

This book is dedicated to Jim Christopher (1957-2023), one of the finest men I've ever known.

TABLE OF CONTENTS

FOREWORD

CAN I BE HONEST WITH YOU?

Before we dive in, I want to be straight with you. If you're looking for advice on how to be more charismatic or win more business using newfound motivational-speaking skills, you bought the wrong book. You know those rah-rah, jump-up-and-down-to-get-you-pumped-to-close-deals guys you see on YouTube? That's not me. Don't get me wrong. People tell me I'm a great speaker. I trained at one of the most intensive and effective public-speaking programs in the country and have worked for decades to improve my craft. But when it comes to selling, I'm much more interested in listening than speaking. More on that in the chapters to come.

No, this isn't yet another refresh of the Dale Carnegie classic *How to Win Friends and Influence People*. Depending on what you know about sales, the stuff I'm going to teach you may sound so counterintuitive you'll want to dropkick this book into the yard. For instance, when I'm meeting with prospects, I love hearing the word "No." I often tell a prospect, "You're probably not ready for me yet," and I'll mean it.

In my years as a sales trainer, coach and consultant, many a salesperson has walked into the office of their boss (my client) and said, "Man, the shit that guy is teaching is crazy. It doesn't make any sense." The fun part is six months later, when that same salesperson tells others, "Not only am I selling more stuff and making more money, but I'm also getting along better with my partner and kids. This No BS Sales System approach has changed my life."

The stuff I teach may scare the hell out of you because it's radically different from everything you know about sales. It requires you to get real with yourself and your prospects.

I'm not afraid to get real. Years ago, early in my career in commercial real estate, I was at the lake one weekend fishing with a buddy, a longtime friend who sold lockers, racking and in-plant offices to industrial buyers.

"Walker," he said, casting a bass lure toward a pine tree that had toppled and was lying half-submerged. "Did I tell you that I hired a guy to help me with sales? A sales trainer. We start next week."

"What? You don't need help selling," I said. "You're like me. You know everybody in town, and you can talk to anybody. You don't need sales training."

"No, I think I do," he said. "I know I can do better, and I need to make more money. My sales are steady, but I haven't grown my book in the last two years. I gotta fix that."

Then he told me the trainer's name and what he was paying him. "Man, I've heard that guy's commercials on the radio. What's he going to teach you that you don't already know?"

Back home, I couldn't stop thinking about my buddy and the crazy idea that he was going to fork over $6,000 of *his money* to get taught something he was already good at.

The idea really got under my skin. I was convinced he was getting scammed.

I'd never had any kind of sales training before. I spent four years at a top Southern liberal arts college, but now I was done with school. I was learning on the job, gaining real-world experience and using my personality and charm to close deals.

Or *try* to close deals. I'd been at it a while, and I wasn't making as much money as I wanted. One reason was the economy. These were tough times in commercial real estate. And there weren't a lot of transactions going on in the small Southern capital city where I lived. Plus, my boss was kind of an asshole. I was definitely not one of his favorites. Hell, the only sales advice I ever got from him was: "You need to be the smartest guy in the room *and* the biggest asshole in the room."

I was pretty good at the second part of that but failed miserably at the first one.

So, I called Matt, the sales-trainer guy.

"My friend Blake gave you a bunch of money, and I gotta be honest: I don't think he needs your help to be better at sales," I told him. "I want to meet you to see what he bought."

Despite my skepticism and confrontational introduction, Matt took the meeting.

We sat down in his office, and the first thing I noticed is that he didn't put much value in small talk. No chatter about who we knew in common or what I thought about the weather. Matt was nice, but not chummy. He was calm but focused. I noticed that he listened intently when I spoke.

"Wow, you're in commercial real estate," he said after a few minutes of getting up to speed. "You probably don't need my help. You must be making a million bucks a year."

"Oh, no," I said.

"Half a million?"

"No way."

"Two-hundred-fifty thousand?"

"Not yet."

"Two hundred thousand?"

"I hope to this year," I said.

"Why not a million?"

I told him about the economy and the soft real-estate market. I told him how hard it is to do commercial deals in a sleepy city like this one. I told him about my asshole boss and how political my company was and that I just didn't play those games. Besides, I had been in the business for only seven years.

I looked up, and Matt was giving me the stop-sign hand gesture. I paused.

"What?"

"Suppose I told you I thought those were . . . excuses," he said, pausing before he said the last word.

I immediately flashed anger.

"What do you mean?" I asked.

"Those are excuses," he said, calmly.

I almost got up to walk out.

But then it hit me like a rock. Those *were* excuses. And no one had ever called me out on that before.

I sat back in the chair to gather myself.

He then followed up with, "Walker, where else are you making excuses in your life?"

I thought, *Damn! I live in a shitty apartment. I'm in debt. I'm 30 years old, and my mom tells me I'm never going to get married because I'm such an asshole.*

The stories I'd been telling myself about why I hadn't been more successful were making me the victim in the story. A victim is powerless. Instead of taking responsibility for my own circumstances, I chose to blame the economy, the marketplace and my boss (who was really a great guy, despite my whining).

I told Matt all this, really opened up to him. Hell, I wept. *He had helped me discover through the questions he asked that I was the problem.* Shit got real.

Matt listened without judgment. He asked a lot of questions that helped me understand that I had been making excuses my entire adult life. No wonder it got under my skin when my buddy told me he'd hired this guy. I had all these problems, but I was hiding them deep inside me, afraid of how I would look to the world if I admitted (even to myself) that I needed to change. It was a tough realization that I was the problem. The good news was that I was also the solution.

I needed Matt's help to address my many issues. Before I left his office that day, I wrote him a check to become a client. Of course, the check bounced—further confirmation that I needed to fix some stuff in my life. I scraped up the money and paid him, and, over the next three years, he helped me. In fact, he changed my life.

His advice eventually led me to start my own commercial real-estate-consulting company. I made a lot more money and ended up referring him a ton of new business.

But hiring Matt was just the start. Once I decided to get real and stop making excuses—a goal that requires constant vigilance and discipline—I set off on a yearslong path of personal and professional growth and learning. That journey led me to create the No BS Sales System and a training and consulting business, the No BS Sales School, to teach others the lessons that had taken me so long to learn.

These lessons helped me get better at sales, and, as a result, I earned more money. This book will help you do the same. But deep down, making more money is not really what the No BS Sales System is all about. More on that in a bit.

When I first told my mother—a smart and kind, straightlaced and very proper Southern Lady—that I was creating a company called "No BS Sales," she winced. I quickly responded by telling her to get her mind out of the gutter—that "No BS" stood for "No Bad Salespeople." But she knew me well enough to know what it really stood for.

I named my approach the No BS Sales System after getting fed up with all the bullshit that goes on between buyers and sellers. You know what I'm talking about. The sales guys who spew information from the marketing brochures—*We've got better products! Better quality! Better service! Blah, blah, blah.* Meanwhile, prospects don't know who to believe, so they gather three different proposals, one each from three different companies. (It must be a rule somewhere that you have to get three.)

Some people just have to choose the lowest price. That's either their directive or their own practice. You don't want this person to pick you. By choosing only the lowest price, he's telling you he puts no value on you. He has commoditized your product. He'll demand the best of everything but want to pay you only the minimum. That guy will be your worst customer.

Other people will pick the middle price. That's safe. They'll think the low-price proposal is probably not as good, and they'd be fools to pick the most expensive. Sometimes they'll give a proposal—full of your free consulting—to their incumbent (the guy who is currently selling to them) and use it to chisel them down on price.

It's like both sides are doing this dance, a dance they've both come to expect, except it's not a dance at all. It's a dysfunctional relationship, marked by a disconnect between buyer and seller and corrosive cynicism. They're two people missing each other, to everyone's detriment.

A buyer may get the best deal on a good or service, but they often don't get what they need because of their flawed process. And a seller will chase and chase prospects who don't respond, believing persistence is the only way to win. Not only are they wasting time and emotional energy, but they're also burning those "relationships" they claim to want so badly. This dysfunctional dance is caused by following the prospect's system. It's a trap, and I'll break it down for you in "Chapter One: Mastering the Mind." Throughout this book, I'll walk you through how to avoid the prospect's system to the benefit of both you and, believe it or not, your prospect.

When I'm a buyer—of a new computer, office space, software or some other high-dollar item—I hate wading through sales BS that makes everyone defensive and wastes my time. As a seller, I refuse to play BS sales games. I've learned that being direct, transparent and real makes selling fun and interesting. By skipping the BS, I close more deals, build more trust, solve more problems for people and feel good about my work and myself.

I'm going to teach you how to do the same.

You get to be honest and direct with your prospects and expect the same back from them. It sounds easy, but it takes work, structure and lots of practice. Consider this book the structure—the blueprint for how to design your own success. The work is up to you.

I call this book *Some Will. Some Won't. So What. Who's Next?* because the title succinctly captures my attitude about sales. With prospects, I want to get to "Yes" or "No" as efficiently as possible. If it's a "No," I want to walk away amicably, no hard feelings, and keep the door open in case they need my help down the road.

Meeting Matt all those years ago helped me get past a major hurdle in my life: my deeply insecure self. I no longer have to have all the answers. I now know that the ability to show weakness is a strength. And I no longer have to make the sale to validate that I am good enough.

It took years of self-work, including mistakes, false starts and dead-ends, for me to reach the point where I feel deeply secure in who I am and what I am worth, regardless of the outcome of a deal. That sense of self-worth is critical to my success as a salesperson, which is just one of the countless roles I play in life. Here's a brief exercise I use to help my clients understand the difference between our true selves and the roles we play.

ROLE PLAY

Think of all the roles you play in your life. You are a son or daughter, and then maybe some combination of sibling, spouse, parent, car guy, knitter, snowskier, practical joker, tailgater, reader, hiker, birdwatcher, mountain biker, baker and so on. My guess is that, if you really tried, and you used the smallest font possible, you could fill all the walls of your house with the multitude of roles you play. Since you're reading this book, you can probably add "salesperson" or at least "wannabe salesperson" to your list of roles.

Now, pretend that you are deep in the woods, on top of a mountain or on a beautiful beach somewhere—wherever your happy place is. You're alone, and everything is perfect. The weather's ideal. You're safe. You have everything you possibly need. You are there for 30 minutes. The only catch? You had to leave your roles behind. All of those traditional ways of describing yourself are gone. All that's left is you at your core.

What is your value now? Stripped of your various roles, what are you worth on a scale of 1 to 10, where one has the lowest value and 10 has the highest? Pick a number.

When I pose this question to groups of salespeople, I get a range of answers.

Some people give themselves low marks, say 1 to 4. I call those people "non-winners." It's not that they can't make money or achieve greatness. They might make a billion dollars a year. They might be well-liked, even famous. But deep down they somehow see themselves as *less than*, and they're desperately afraid somebody will figure it out. The non-winners are often the most arrogant among us, because they shield themselves with false bravado. They believe there's only so much success in the world. They'll tear other people down or create chaos in others' lives to lift themselves up.

Then you've got the folks in the middle—5 to 7. I call these the "at-leasters." They found their comfort zone. They'll say, "Well, I'm not doing great, but at least I'm better than Joe over there." They measure themselves against others, and when others are doing better, the at-leasters have excuses as to why. If they ever perform above their average, they will think it was a fluke: "I'm good, but I'm not that good." They average themselves back down. That was me when I first did this exercise. I ranked myself a 6 out of 10. I had a million reasons why I wasn't the highest performer and a desperate fear of being outdone by those I believed were below me. I was the king of the comfort zone.

At the top—8, 9, 10—are the "winners." They have a strong belief that things will work out for them. They realize that not only is it okay to fail, but failure is inevitable if you're growing and changing. Winners are often the humblest people. No matter their skill or achievement level, they know they could always be better and are striving to be so. Winners believe they were meant to lift other people up. They see that there are unlimited amounts of success in the world, and they want others to experience it. Their world is filled with opportunities for success, and helping others is part of who they are.

Then I surprise people with the real point of the exercise: Everybody is a 10. The problem is that most people don't realize they are.

It's my belief that, for billions of years before any of us ever existed, there has been a being that loves all of us 100% and will continue to do so for eternity. It is from that divine love that all of your true worth is derived. This is your core, your self-worth, and it does not need validation from anyone or any achievement. You are full and complete, no matter your circumstances.

Picture a seed in the ground. Its value is a 10. It sprouts a little green shoot, and its value is a 10. It grows into a plant that blooms and is a 10. Eventually it dies and goes back into the ground as fertilizer for other plants, and its value is still a 10.

Humans complicate things a bit. With self-knowledge comes self-doubt. We have roles; some we choose, and some are chosen for us.

When your mother discovered you in her womb, you landed your first role as baby. In time, you are born and begin to take on roles like son or daughter, cousin, happy baby or colicky baby, and then toddler, maybe sibling and so on. The older you grow, the more roles you pick up, like student, artist, golfer, dancer, gamer, botanist, beer drinker, athlete, fashionista. Then maybe you have a family and career, and your number of roles increases exponentially. The more roles you pick up, the more value you and those around you place on those roles rather than on who you are at your core.

Why does that matter? One reason is that everybody has ups and downs in their roles. Maybe you lost a big sale you were counting on, or an important relationship has gone bad. Or maybe you got fired. All of those things suck. One of my favorite sayings is by a guy named Steve Sims. He says, "Nobody drowns from falling into the water. They drown from failing to get out." It matters not that you fail, but what you do next. A 10 knows that, while we can't control what happens, we can control how we react. We are not victims.

Everyone is a 10, only most don't know it.

So, what does all this have to do with sales?

Everything.

Good selling is having someone trust you enough to give you money to make a problem go away. Most of the people you talk to are not going to buy from you, especially at first. You're going to hear "No" a lot more than "Yes." By knowing that your true value does not come from sales made or lost, you can remain emotionally objective and not take rejection personally.

How would you treat everyone around you if you knew that they were all 10s, the same as you, no better, no worse?

Most people I ask say, "With respect."

Two people I used to use as examples of being 10s, or winners, that I now know are 1s (non-winners) are Lance Armstrong and Tiger Woods. Both exhibited signs of being 10s, like a desire for constant improvement and willingness to take risks. And, man—did they take risks! The risks that they took, however, caused chaos and pain to those around them. They showed a lack of empathy and respect for the people who were closest to them.

Respect for all is the essence of the No BS Sales System. We respect ourselves by understanding that we're not right for everyone and that we have equal business stature with everyone we meet. We respect our prospects by asking and not telling, and by being a guide and not a hero. I'll say more about those beliefs in Chapter One under "Mindset Makeovers."

When I have a problem in my life or work, I'm a buyer looking for solutions. Ideally, I want to work with someone I trust—someone who's trying to understand what I really need to solve my true problem, someone with *my* best interests in mind. If you want to be that person to your prospects and clients, then this book will help you get there. Whether you're selling tractors, surgical instruments or commercial insurance, this book can teach you to be that trusted guide to your clients.

Most of my clients come to me with the goal of closing more deals to make more money. They achieve their goal by becoming the best version of themselves: fearless and bold, yet empathetic and deeply interested in other people. They'll say, "Holy shit! This is so much bigger than sales. I got better at sales, but I also learned to eliminate excuses in my life and communicate better with other people. I learned to tell the truth all the time and help people share the truth with me, making them a better version of themselves."

I love that. Those are the people I'm looking for. They're not the "check-the-box, I've-done-sales-training" types. They put their heart into it. They have a personal compelling reason why they need to make a change. Getting to work with people like that has been one of the greatest rewards of my life. In this book, I'll teach you how to identify those people in your own business and rule out the ones who aren't committed to change.

Back when I was in the commercial real-estate business— before I met Matt, the sales coach—I rode to the beach one weekend with a buddy of mine who was in the same business. Even though we started around the same time, he was making about three times more money than me. I've never been shy about speaking up, so one day I asked him: "You close more deals than I do. You make two or three times the money I'm making. What do you think the difference between us is?"

"I'll tell you what it is, Walker," he said. "My dad died when I was young. My mom cleaned schools at night to support us. I paid my way through college. I have a wife and two kids. Three years ago, we lived in a trailer, but I recently built a house. I know that if I don't make what I need to make, we'll have to move back into that damn trailer. I've got no options."

All I could do was nod my head.

"You?" he said. "You're always looking for the better deal. You look for the easier path. If worse comes to worst, you have a family that will support you."

That was true. My family wasn't wealthy, but my dad wasn't going to let me starve—or move into a mobile home.

"I'm committed, and you're playing around," he said. He didn't say this with anger or spite. He was being truthful.

Still, his words pissed me off for about three months, but, eventually, I realized he was right. I think that's another reason why I got so emotional when Matt called me out for making excuses. Deep down, I knew he was right.

I learned that, to truly change, I needed to stop making excuses and commit to not being the victim I'd become.

You're reading this book for a reason. You're investing in yourself. This book didn't cost you much, but if you want to get better at sales, the job that feeds your family, you need to commit the time and effort. This book is not for motivation. That's on you. If you're not already motivated to become a better, more-successful salesperson, put this book down now, or, better yet, give it to someone else who is.

But if you are motivated to get better at sales, this book will give you the blueprint for how to do it. Turn the page and find out.

❖ ❖ ❖

INTRODUCTION

THE PROSPECT'S TRAP

When I say the word "salesperson," what personality traits come to mind? Not to describe you or anyone you trust and respect but, you know, other "salespeople." My guess is that you'll come up with words like "cheesy" or "pushy"—maybe even "liar." How else would you describe a typical salesperson? *Talks too much? Super positive? Overly (and sometimes creepily) friendly? Full of shit?*

These days, people have a natural inclination to be wary that they're being sold. "Really?" they think. "That guy is probably full of shit. How does he know what I need? He's only out to sell me something." Or, "Everybody says the same damn thing. Everybody says theirs is the best. How in the hell am I supposed to know?"

By doing sales the way you've always done it, you're creating a low-trust environment, where everything you say is scrutinized by your prospect.

The prospect's wariness is a challenge for everyone in sales. I believe that good selling is having someone trust you enough to give you money to make a problem go away. To create that trusting relationship with your prospect, you'll first need to understand the prospect's brain.

Most prospects have learned to manipulate salespeople to get what they want. Most sellers use an outdated sales approach that allows and sometimes even encourages the manipulation. See if you recognize yourself in the following example.

THE PROSPECT'S BRAIN

I was on a call not long ago with a prospect named Jeff, a young financial planner who was exploring ways to boost his bottom line.

"Tell me about the last time you thought you had made a sale, but it blew up," I said to Jeff.

"That's easy," he said. "Last month, I got introduced to a guy and went to meet him. I explained what I did, asked some questions about the problems he was having and told him how I thought I could fix them."

Jeff said the guy was very interested in what he had to say and asked if Jeff could put together a proposal for how he would solve his financial conundrum.

"I told him, 'Sure, I'd love to do that,'" Jeff said.

Jeff told me he went back to his office, pored over his meeting notes and spent four to five hours writing up a plan. He later met with the guy and his wife (which he took as a good sign!) a second time and walked him through the steps and what it would cost in fees.

"At the end of the meeting," Jeff said, "the guy told me, 'This really looks great. You've done a beautiful job. You understand where I'm trying to go.'" But moving their assets to Jeff was a big decision, they said, and they wanted to think it over for a while, maybe a week.

"I thought that made perfect sense," said Jeff, agreeing to call back in a week. At that point, he was pretty pumped. "The guy seemed excited, and I thought we got along well. Hell, the wife said she wanted me to come to their house to have dinner sometime!"

"On Friday, I picked up the phone to follow up. I didn't want to seem too eager," Jeff told me, "so I waited till around 11 o'clock. I called and got his voicemail. I didn't think much of it because, you know, people are busy."

"Good. What message did you leave?" I asked.

"Oh, the usual: 'Hey, this is Jeff from XYZ wealth management. I'm calling you back to see if you've decided anything about the financial plan. I'd love to work with you. Call me back.'"

"When he called you back, what did he say?" I asked.

"He didn't call me back."

"Okay, makes sense," I said to Jeff. "So you called back a few days later?"

"Yep," he said. "I got voicemail again, so I left another message."

"But that time, he called you back. . . ."

"Nope," said Jeff, his voice sinking.

"By the way, how much would that deal have been worth for you?" I asked.

"About $11,000 a year."

"How long do you hope to keep a client like that?"

"Around 20 years," Jeff said.

"So, 20 times 11. I'm not very good at math. How much is that?" I asked.

"It's 220 grand," he said, sounding frustrated.

"And how often does something like that happen?"

"It happens all the time," he said. "Maybe around three or four times a month. It's not just me. It seems to happen to other people in the office all the time, too. I was taught the Golden Rule: 'He with the gold rules.' It's just going to happen."

"Okay, here's what I heard you say," I replied. "Tell me what I've missed when I'm done. You meet with a prospect and try to educate them on what you do and how you can help. You talk about your investment philosophy, some features and benefits about your firm and how you work. You ask some questions—you know, things like how much in investable assets they have now, how they're invested and maybe some goals they might have for their money.

"They don't share a ton of information with you during that first meeting because they barely know you, but they ask you a lot of questions, including about fees. They're really nice to you. At the end of the meeting, they ask you to create a financial plan with the information they've provided you. At that point, you go spend half a day and create a plan that should get them where they want to be. You schedule another meeting and go over the plan.

"Now they're a little more open and fill in the gaps of information you needed. Things seem to be going well. His spouse, who you requested be there, is great and seems to trust you. She says she wants to invite you over for dinner! But they need to think it over. And they ask you to call them back in a week. And when you do, you get voicemail—three times. And they never call you back. It's like they've disappeared," I said. "So, what did I miss?"

"That's exactly what happened," Jeff said.

I asked: "Jeff, who is in control when you sell like that?"

"Well," he stammered, "I guess the prospect is."

"You're right," I said. "But do you know why the prospect is in control?"

"No," he said, looking dejected. "But I'm guessing you're gonna tell me."

"Only if you want me to," I offered.

"Hell, yeah. Tell me what I'm missing," he said, perking up a bit.

"Jeff, the prospect is following a system that allows them to keep control of the sale, and you're letting it happen. If it makes you feel any better, I bet 99% of salespeople make the same mistake. Some consciously allow it. Others have no idea it's happening. The good news is that it's a fixable problem."

THE STANDARD SELLER'S PROCESS

Chances are, if you've been in sales for any time at all, Jeff's story sounds familiar. Maybe that's how you were taught. Millions of salespeople have been trained to be nice, find things in common with their prospect, share the features and benefits of what they sell, give a written proposal, overcome any objections, do a trial close and then ask for the business. If the prospect doesn't buy then, you set an appointment to follow up, and you're persistent in your efforts to re-engage and close them.

People have been trained to sell this way for more than 80 years. And many have been very successful using this methodology. Even if you've never had training, you've probably learned this process from watching other people sell or maybe even from being sold to yourself. For many people, the way Jeff was selling is simply what sales looks like. It's just what it is.

But there's a big problem with this methodology: Everyone knows it, including your prospects. Humans are smart. Our ancestors (or some of them, anyway) learned to recognize patterns that signified danger and either adapt or perish. Since most of us don't have to fear sabertooth tigers anymore, we're able to look for patterns that might show a much-less-deadly-but-still-ominous being, the salesperson. That no-good, fast-talking, sleazy salesperson who's trying to trick us into buying! I'm being dramatic, of course, but remember how you might have described "those other salespeople" at the beginning of the chapter.

Your prospects are mostly cynical about salespeople. Many try to educate themselves about any product or service before they talk to you or any other seller. When asked why they do this, prospects say things like "All salespeople are liars" or "I don't want them to waste my time."

Before Al Gore invented the internet, salespeople were the gatekeepers of information. You had to go to someone like us to get information and pricing. That's probably why, many years ago, if you could be a nice-enough person and had a decent product, you'd probably make a decent living.

Not any more, though. Information is free and can be gotten instantaneously. Pricing, terms, specs, comparisons, competitors—everything is available for free at the touch of a couple of keystrokes on a smartphone. Many believe that a salesperson is not only *not* helpful but is also a roadblock to getting what they want for the price they want to pay. Prospects have developed their own systems for counteracting your outdated system. They've learned to take power and control from you. You end up doing free consulting, chasing people to no avail and ultimately wasting your time. And can you blame them? Sure, but blaming them is an excuse.

By believing they're the problem, you're saying you're powerless to fix it. I'm here to help you stop blaming them and give you the tools to fix the only thing you control: you.

Here's the four-step prospect system being used against you that's making you lose control over your interactions. The prospect will first:

1. Ask about the price.

It's the only thing they can compare, no matter their expertise (or lack thereof) on what you sell. This can sound like anything from "If you can do it cheaper than I'm getting it now . . ." to "How much are you asking for. . . ." This is the first hurdle you'll have to jump. If you make it past price, then the prospect will:

2. Get free consulting.

Now you're "invited in." This can be anything from being invited to have a longer phone conversation, to meeting them at their office or place of business, to them showing up over Webex for a demo. Often the prospect will be super friendly and nice. They'll ask you questions. You'll spend all the time they want answering those questions. They'll be very interested. They'll give you scenarios and ask you how what you do would help. They'll smile. They will ask you to put all that in writing. You will interpret this as "We're building a relationship" and "These are buying signals," which will make you very excited.[1] You will rush to get them the proposal/information, including price. If it takes multiple meetings, you will smartly set up a time to go over the proposal with them. At this point, they will:

3. Say nice things and get rid of you.

Once you give that proposal, you'll do a "trial close" and be battle-ready to "overcome objections." If they don't buy here, they'll tell you things like: "This really looks good. I am almost certain that what you have is what we need. Thank you so much for taking so much time to explain. Apples to apples,[2] all things considered, I don't see any reason we wouldn't give y'all a shot." And then they'll make the killer comment: "This is a big decision, of course. I'm going to need to think about it for a couple of days." Or maybe, "My partner is traveling in Europe, and I'll need to run it by her." Or, "I'll need to run this by the CFO." Or, "My board is going to have to sign off on this, but they always let me do what I want." Or, "I've still got a few more proposals I'll need to look over." You get the point.

They'll wrap up with: "Why don't you call me in a week (or next month) and we can get this all squared away?"

At this point, you are still excited because they said nice things. You can feel the relationship blossoming. You can already see the two of you having dinner together and being lifelong friends. Until they:

---

[1] The only buying signal is a check and a signed contract. Don't be a dope.
[2] Whenever someone gives you the "fruit analogy," it's another time you're about to not get paid.

4. Disappear.

Your boss asks you about the deal, and you tell her it's looking good. You're supposed to call the prospect back in a week to get the contract signed. You put it at 90% in the CRM.

So, now you wait. It usually happens that "a week from now" is a Friday. I don't know why. Maybe it's a law? Anyway, Friday comes, and you begin negotiating with yourself about when to actually make the call. *Don't want to call too early and seem too eager. . . . Don't want to call too late on a Friday because they might be gone. . . .* And eventually you land on some time between 11:00 and 11:30. (*Can't call after 11:30, because they might be at lunch.*)

Ask any phone rep about the call volume on Fridays between 11:00 and 11:30 a.m., and I bet they'll tell you it spikes during that time.

Expectations are high! Getting this one done will make it easy to roll into the weekend. So you make the call. And the phone rings.

And your prospect sees your name pop up on his phone. Since the last time you met, he took your information from the proposal and gave it to his incumbent or one of your competitors (with the price blacked out, of course.) You told him $100, but he tells the others you said $90. Then he says, "If you can beat this, we can do business."

Or, maybe he gets two other quotes. (*Gotta get three quotes!*) That must be another law. Anyway, all three sellers send in a proposal with their specs and information. They will all tell the prospect that they, in fact, have better service, better people and a product that's a better value. Those are their differentiators. All of them have the same differentiators.

And they all put the price on the last page so the prospect has to read their whole document to see the difference!

So the prospect skips all the fluff, flips to the back page and looks at the price.

One comes in at $100 (you).

One comes in at $82.

The last comes in at $89.

The prospect now has a choice: "Hmmm. I'd be stupid to pick the highest price, even though it does look like it could be better. The low price is probably a bad choice. Maybe I should pick the one in the middle."

All of this has been going on in the background while you've been waiting patiently to call back.

Your name pops up on your prospect's phone.

He thinks: "Damn! It's the salesperson I'm not going to buy anything from. He's a nice guy, but I don't want to tell him I've gone in another direction." And he sends you to voicemail.

You get voicemail, and your heart dies a little. You leave a nice message like, "Hey, John. I hope you're well. Calling you back about the proposal we talked about last week. I know your partner was out of town and you needed to talk to her. Let me know if you have any questions. I'll keep my phone with me, so feel free to call. I'm around all weekend. Talk soon!"

He doesn't call back.

Being persistent, you decide to call him back on Monday afternoon, knowing how busy everyone is on Monday morning. You dial.

His phone rings, and he sees it's you again. "Ugh. I really don't want to hurt his feelings, but I don't want to ruin his day," he thinks and sends you to voicemail again.

And you get voicemail. And your heart dies a little bit more. And you leave another cheery message, "Hey, John. Hope you had a nice weekend. Sorry I missed you last Friday. I wanted to see if you had any questions. We're excited to get started working with you, but I need that contract signed. Call me back. Okay—hope you're well."

And the prospect sees you've left another message and deletes it without listening.

It's now Thursday of the week after you gave him the information. Your boss is hassling you because he wants you to get this sale done before the end of the month so he can make his numbers. "Be persistent," he repeats, ad nauseam.

So, you call once more.

And the prospect sees it's you again. This time he's irritated. "This guy is driving me crazy! Why does he keep calling me??? He's an idiot. I'm not going to buy from him. He needs to leave me alone!!!"

Once again, you go to voicemail.

This time your heart has about had it. You are consumed by frustration and desperation at the same time. You leave one more voice message: "Hey, John. Sorry we keep missing each other. I talked to my boss, and we may be able to work out some kind of discount for you if we get this done by the end of the month. Call me back, please . . ."

Has this ever happened to you?

Here's a better question: Have you ever done this to someone else?

Of course, you have.

Who wins in this scenario?

Not the seller, for sure.

Not the prospect, either, because they either picked the middle-priced guy or beat up the incumbent who promised to do all that you said you would do but at a price where they can't deliver it.

And probably not the person who got the business, because they had to cut all the margin out of their deal to keep or get the business.

Whether your prospects are consciously following this process or not, you still end up wasting a lot of time—for you and your prospects. Left to their own devices, people don't understand how to buy what you have. And how could they? They've been trained by crappy salespeople who are happy to vomit information and sell based on price. In the end, nobody wins.

Chances are, you're reading this book because you're looking for a different approach. I will teach you that approach—the No BS Sales System—but it's not enough to understand the prospect's mind. You must also know your own mind—and heart—and be open to making some elemental changes in how you view the world.

❖ ❖ ❖

CHAPTER ONE

MASTERING THE MIND

To avoid the prospect's trap, we need to follow a system that can give us 50% control of the sales process. Under the prospect's system, the scales are tipped against you; prospects demand free consulting and then use your information against you before they ghost you. If the power imbalance favored you, you might say, "You'll buy my company's widget at a 1,000% markup and we won't pick up the phone when you need product support." What client would go for that? We need a system that is equitable, where both prospect and seller can be truthful and transparent, where both know that, at every step, they have the opportunity and obligation to say "No" and part with no hard feelings or "Yes" and take the next step forward.

To implement this new system, however, you must first change the mindsets that got you there in the first place. By examining your current beliefs and then identifying which ones are no longer helpful, you can not only understand the prospect's mind but also frame your own mindset to develop a healthier and more productive attitude when selling.

A mentor of mine once told me, "Walker, don't believe everything you think." So much of how we see the world began when we were children. Were you ever told: "Don't cross the street!" or, "Don't talk to strangers"? Or maybe, "For God's sake, don't talk about money"? Those and other rules kept you safe as a child and your parents from being embarrassed, but, at some point, you needed to ditch those rules. The same goes for certain generally accepted mindsets that can severely limit your success in sales.

MINDSET MAKEOVERS

I'm going to lay out four mindsets you need to shed—and four mindsets you should replace them with to successfully use the No BS Sales System.

MINDSET MAKEOVER #1

Shed: Everybody is a prospect.
Adopt: You're not the right fit for everybody.

You start a sales job, learn the features and benefits of your product or service, and then begin to believe that everyone in a certain business category "needs" what you have. I mean, they'd be stupid not to buy this, right? "It makes so much sense," you say to yourself. You become an evangelist for what you sell and want to tell as many people as possible about how great it is. An evangelist wants to save everyone. The easy ones are those who say they don't want to be saved. They'll just tell you "No" or not take your calls. The harder ones are the ones that meet with you, ask a lot of questions, get your information in writing and say nice things—but aren't a good fit.

Why not? Maybe they're happy with what they have. Maybe they're under contract or some other obligation that keeps them from changing. Maybe it's not a priority now for them to fix the problem you so perfectly solve. Maybe they don't have any money. Maybe they can buy only if you're the cheapest option. Maybe they're assholes, and it wouldn't be worth your time to help them.

There are lots of reasons someone's not going to be the right fit. The sooner you identify those reasons and disqualify those people, the better!

Chasing prospects who aren't ready, willing and able to make a change is a waste of your time. As a matter of fact, chasing prospects at all is a complete waste of time. Not everyone is ready for what you have to offer. Not everyone deserves a proposal. Even some of those who ask for a proposal don't deserve one. There is very little upside to giving your information—pricing, terms, descriptions, etc.—to prospects who aren't ready or able to make a yes-or-no decision. When you recognize that a prospect is not qualified to receive the solutions you might have for them, I give you full permission to tell that prospect: "I'm afraid I'd only be wasting your time by giving this information to you right now."

One thing to keep in mind: Your prospect's world changes every 90 days, just like yours does. Think back to 90 days ago. What were you focused on? My guess is that it's probably not the same as right now. In another 90 days, things will be different again. Just because someone isn't ready for you now doesn't mean it'll be that way forever. You're in this for the long haul. Keep moving.

Ten years ago, I met with a guy who ran an electrical-supply company. They had eight salespeople. I called him out of the blue when prospecting, and he said that he definitely had a sales problem. He told me his team didn't prospect for new business and were only making sales when someone asked for something—"order takers," he called them. When I asked, he said he figured it was costing him more than $1 million in sales a year and probably $400k in bottom-line revenue. He told me if he could grab that additional revenue, he'd be able to buy his wife the beach house she'd always wanted. I asked him when he hoped to fix the problem. He said, "Not until next year." It was February.

"Why next year?" I asked.

"Because I want to buy my partner out at a lower price, based on current revenues," he said. "My wife can wait."

There was no reason to tell him how much it would cost to work with me or explain how I could help him. He wasn't ready.

I'm lucky that I've put myself in a position to be really picky about who I take as a client. If my gut says "Nah," I trust that feeling. I want you to get your business to the same place.

I did meet with him the following year, and, while he still had that million-dollar problem, I decided he wasn't someone I wanted to work with.

Now, we've talked about people who aren't ready for you yet—or just aren't the right fit—but what about customers who aren't the right size?

Here's a story I heard a long time ago:

A man and his family move deep into the woods. He knows there are a lot of squirrels nearby that would be a good food source. On the first day, he gets up in the morning, grabs a gun and goes squirrel hunting. He walks all day and returns home with half a dozen of the furry little varmints. He skins, cleans and cooks them. The next day, he sets out again, walks all day and returns with five squirrels, which he skins, cleans and cooks for his family. Each day he repeats the process, but he soon finds that he has to walk farther and farther to find enough squirrels to feed his family. *This sucks*, he thinks. *My feet hurt. My family isn't getting enough to eat. And I'm sick of squirrel stew.*

Tired of this grind, he decides to do something different. "I'm going to kill an elephant," he says. "Then I can feed my family for two years." So, he gathers his gear and sets out.

A couple of days go by, and the man still isn't back. The son thinks, *Shit, I'm hungry. We don't know when dad is coming back. There aren't any elephants nearby. He's as likely to get killed by one as kill one himself. How in the hell would he even drag one back?* And then the son spies a deer.

That afternoon, the son grabs his rifle, climbs a tree and shoots a deer. He drags the deer home, skins it, cleans it and has enough food to feed his family for two weeks. He goes out again 10 days later, shoots another deer and keeps the family fed for another two weeks. Meanwhile, the father is still out trying to kill an elephant.

You already know where this story is going. No big surprises here. Think of your prospects and clients as squirrels, deer and elephants.

On the surface, there's nothing wrong with any of them.

The squirrels are your smaller clients or customers. Maybe you started your business with them. You were just glad to have the business! You may make big margins on squirrels, but you aren't making much money. (Margins of 100% on $100 for most folks is just not that much money, unless you're doing tremendous volume.) The problem is that squirrels are needy! They need a lot of service and handholding. One sign that you have a book full of squirrels is that you're always afraid you're going to run out of time.

At the other end of the spectrum, you have the elephants, which are your big clients or largest prospects. Define them as any one customer who makes up more than 25% of your revenues. Elephants take a long time to close, and you probably have to make a lot of concessions to get the deal. You need to staff up to handle the business. You have to customize your services to suit them. One of my clients likens closing a deal with an elephant to buying a boat. The first day is the best day. It's all downhill from there!

The life cycle of an elephant looks like this. First comes the excitement of closing the deal. "This client will be a gamechanger," you tell yourself. You'll either hire more staff or divert current staff to handle the account. Soon after you get started, the client will ask that you do a few extra things for them, but without additional compensation. This is called "scope creep." You agree, of course, to build goodwill and improve the "relationship." Your margins are getting a little thin, but the revenues are good, so you justify it and keep moving. At this point, as far as you know, things are going great! You are spending a whole lot of time managing the account to make sure it continues to go well, but it's worth it to maintain the relationship.

And then, at some point in the future—maybe it's six months, maybe two years—you get a call from your elephant that sounds something like this: "Hey, Susan. Just want to tell you how much we love working with you. I really appreciate the relationship. We've got a problem, though. One of your competitors has contacted us and has offered to do what you're doing for us for a lot less money. My board/boss is putting lots of pressure on me to reduce costs. I'm having to review everything, including our agreement with you. This is really hard. I'd rather work with you, but I'm going to need you to cut your fees by 20%."

How would you handle this call?

Here's how most people handle it: "Sure. We'll be happy to cut our prices to match the competitor." (You know, because of the relationship.)

Now you're doing the same work as before but with no margin. It's harder to pay your staff, and it's damn near impossible to deliver the same service. Plus, you're probably a little resentful that you're caught in this trap: You can't fire them because you depend on the revenue, but it's hard to give them the service they demand now that the account is no longer profitable.

The next thing that happens is you get fired because "your service isn't what it used to be, and they've found another vendor who can handle the work for even less money." And the cycle repeats.

Now you're really screwed because you haven't had time to prospect for new business in a long time; you've ignored the clients in your sweet spot because they weren't asking for much, and now you're not in a good place to ask for referrals from them. You're in panic mode because a huge chunk of your revenue is gone.

Many companies do not survive when an elephant leaves.

As you read this story, does any customer or client come to mind? Or former customer or client?

My guess is, if you've been in business for any time at all, you've probably experienced the damage an elephant can do.

Then there are the deer. These are the ones in the middle. Right in your sweet spot. There are probably hundreds of them in your marketplace, if not thousands. They're easy to find. They can use your product or service without lots of modifications or specialization. They're not very needy. And you can make good money by working with them.

Everyone's business is different, but if you had somewhere between, say, 20 and 100 deer, you'd have a damn nice business, I bet.

As a rule of thumb, 15% of your business will go away every year. Some clients will outgrow you. Some will go out of business. Some will get bought. Maybe you'll mess one up bad enough that they'll fire you. It's just business, right?

If you're not adding 15% new to the top line every year, you're going be falling behind.

The message here is: Focus on your deer. Prospect for them, market to them and create products and services that are designed for them. That's where the money is and where you'll find the most satisfaction.

I hope that, over time, your definition of a deer changes and grows. I hope that what seems like an elephant today is a deer tomorrow, or at least in the next five years.

If you have an elephant in your book now, don't panic. You don't have to fire them. Recognize them for what they are: a temporary boost in revenue that takes a lot of energy to service and will one day go away. Keep prospecting. Find and close more deer business so the elephant's impact on your business is lessened.

Making sure your clients are the right fit also benefits when it comes to referrals. People typically can effectively refer you to other businesses/opportunities like themselves or smaller. If you have a book full of squirrels, chances are you're getting mostly referrals to more squirrels. Deer, though, will beget more deer. Elephants won't refer because they know you can't handle more business. So, market to deer, ask your deer clients for referrals to others like them and focus your prospecting efforts on getting more and slightly larger deer.

It's okay to keep an elephant or two in your pipeline, but establish boundaries you're not willing to cross when you engage with them.

Remember, *you're not the right fit for everybody*. You get to dictate the terms and conditions that you're willing to accept, not the other way around.

Your current client base plus your pipeline of new, qualified prospects is your lifeline. The better suited your current clients are for your business model and the more qualified deer you have in your pipeline, the pickier you can be about who you take on and under what terms.

You're probably saying to yourself, "Where the hell am I going to get the time to cultivate all these new deer prospects?"

It's easy: Raise prices on your squirrels. Double or triple them if necessary. Yes, some, if not most, will leave. That's okay. If you keep them at the same terms at the expense of your growth, you're the problem, not them. Others will decide to stay, expand their relationship with you and be willing to pay more for what you provide. Here's an idea: Refer the most-needy squirrels to your worst competitor. Let them choke that guy's business and distract him from calling on your best clients.

I know what you're thinking: "But Walker, those squirrels can grow into deer!" And you're right—a few may. Here's the other side of that, though: If you helped them when they were small, there's a good chance they'll think they've outgrown you when they get bigger and will move on to your competitor, who's been telling them, "We should talk when you get to _____ size."

If you're focused on disqualifying prospects that aren't ready, willing and able to make a change (more on that later), and you're actively prospecting to and prioritizing those prospects that are the right fit, your business will thrive.

One last thing to consider about your prospects and customers: How do they treat you?

How many of your clients always cause drama, don't appreciate you or your staff, don't pay on time or are always bitching and complaining?

It's a hard lesson, but you've taught your clients and customers how to treat you. You've accepted their bad behavior, and they'll treat you like their worst customers treat them. It's never too late to attempt to retrain them. It takes guts to make a stand. You have to be willing to lose them if they won't change.

Remember, *you're not the right fit for everybody.*

I had a public-relations agency as a client a couple of years ago. The agency's largest client by far was a West Coast technology company, whose CEO knew how important his business was to my client, the PR firm. Not only was this guy extremely demanding and rude, but he would demean the staff at the PR firm constantly.

As an example, this psychopath of a CEO would call every week and scream and yell at the people in charge of his account about anything even slightly out of order. He would look for stuff to complain about and seemed to get off on making the employees break down and cry. A couple times a year, he would fly to town for in-person meetings and demand that my client take him to the most expensive restaurant in town. He would order several entrees and then a couple of bottles of the most expensive bottles of wine, taking the unconsumed food and wine back to his room. He didn't care. She was going to pay the bill.

When I learned about this guy, I said, "You have to fire him. This is bullshit. You and your employees are getting abused." The hits to morale and employee turnover came with real business costs. Not to mention the message she was sending her employees: *My clients, no matter how they act, are more important than you, my employees.*

"Why do you put up with this bullshit?" I asked.

"He's my biggest client. There's nothing I can do about it," she said.

"That's the problem," I said. "That's why you have to go find new clients."

In the short term, I advised her how to stand up to this bully by first saying something like, "John, I need to talk to you. The way we are working together now is no longer acceptable. I don't like the way you're treating my employees, and I don't like the way you are treating me and this company. The way I see it, we have a couple of options. I can either refer you to somebody else, or we can set ground rules for how we treat each other and each other's employees."

I checked in with her a couple of weeks later and learned she hadn't made any changes and refused even to stand up for her employees. That's when we parted ways. I told her I couldn't help her. She wasn't taking my advice, and it was too painful to watch.

BEWARE THE BARGAIN HUNTER

Unless your business model is to be the "low-cost provider," be careful about taking on a client whose sole criterion is low price. How do you recognize bargain hunters? The most obvious "tell" is a singular focus on low price during conversations.

Most folks whose only concern is low cost are putting no value on you and the service you provide. They don't care about any other kind of differentiation. Chances are, they'll also be your biggest pain in the ass. They often want your product or service for the lowest price, and then demand the highest service. They're more likely to bitch and whine not only during the sale but also afterwards, when they're not happy with what they got. Bargain hunting can be a red flag. *You're not the right fit for everybody.*

MINDSET MAKEOVER #2

Shed: Convince them to buy.
Adopt: Ask, don't tell.

A doctor does not write a prescription until he has completed a full diagnosis. In the same vein, you should avoid telling people what they need until you fully understand their situation. This is why you should get rid of the mindset that selling is convincing people to buy or "educating them." The only educating that needs to happen is you getting educated on your prospect's situation and what they think about it.

Raise your hand if you're surprised that a book about sales suggests asking more questions. Every salesperson has heard "Ask more questions" more times than they can count. I had a boss years ago who constantly told me that I needed to ask "the right questions" but gave me no clues as to what the right questions were. I switched companies and was advised to ask open-ended questions—you know, the ones that begin with *who, what, where, when, why* and *how.*

Okay, so now I had a track to run on, but I was still not convinced I knew the "right questions." Open-ended questions were getting me facts and data, but I also knew people make changes emotionally first, and then justify their decisions intellectually. Data was important, but I needed to tap into emotions with my questions. I needed to understand people's opinions of the data they shared. "We're growing at 10%" is a nice data point. I want to know "What should that growth rate be?" and then "How did you come up with that number?"

"We close 85% of the opportunities we quote," is, again, a nice data point, but I want to know if they think that's good or bad. Unless they tell you it's a problem, you can't label it as a problem.[3] Believe it or not, in most situations, anything above

---

[3] Your opinions don't matter, especially now, early in the conversation.

about a 50% closing rate is not a good sign. It usually means that either, 1) you're not in front of enough new prospects, or, 2) you're not charging enough money.

Understand your prospect first by asking them questions and gathering *their* opinions before sharing your ideas with them. That's one critical way you'll set yourself apart from the competition.

TALKING POINTS: LET THEM FIGURE IT OUT

There are different ways to convey how much you know. Asking questions lets your prospect (or whomever you're talking to) realize you're knowledgeable on a subject without your having to tell them. Remember, their opinions are more valuable than yours. Let it be their idea how much you know.

I was interviewing a sales guy a couple of years ago and asked him what he did for fun. He said he was a cyclist. I asked him if he was primarily a mountain biker or road biker.

"Road biker," he said.

"Cool. How many miles a week do you ride?"

"About a hundred," he said.

"That is awesome. What kind of bike do you have? Aluminum or carbon frame?" I asked.

"A Specialized S-Works with a carbon frame."

"Bad-ass," I said. I then asked him about the wheels, and he said, "They came with some mid-grade Bontragers, but I'm hoping to upgrade to Zipps when I get the money."

"Hell, yeah," I said. "The Bontragers are excellent, but the Zipps are amazing. And they totally look bad-ass."

See, I didn't have to tell him that I knew about bikes. He just understood because of the questions I asked. By asking questions instead of simply saying, "Hey, I ride bikes too," you put the spotlight on them and encourage them to share more. When you're in front of your prospect, it's vital that you understand them and help them articulate their situation clearly as opposed to attempting to dazzle them with bullshit or even search for things in common, like so many "natural born" salespeople attempt to do.

One part of asking and not telling is never assuming you already know or understand a situation. Don't assume you understand a person's journey or why they do what they do without first digging to find out.

I have a dear friend whose house caught on fire a dozen years ago. Thankfully, he and his family escaped unharmed. He called 911 as they ran down the stairs to get out. Twenty minutes later, fire trucks roared up, dumped thousands of gallons of water on his house and eventually extinguished the fire. My friend spent the next three years fighting with his insurance company over who was going to pay for what. The company had a far different view about what was salvageable and what wasn't.

It was a disaster, in more ways than one.

"Walker," he told me. "The next time my house catches on fire, I'm going to get my family out safely, I'm going to walk the two and a half miles to your house, and I'm going to have two drinks with you. And then I'll call 911. I'm gonna let that f*cker burn to the ground."

I tell this story not to recommend this particular course of action should your own house catch fire, but rather to illustrate how easily our assumptions can turn out wrong. Had I not known the first story and a second fire happened, my advice would have been to call the fire department as quickly as possible to put the fire out. I would have assured him that his insurance company would take care of him. Because he holds a different view based on his particular personal experience, had I made that recommendation, he could easily come to the conclusion that I didn't know what the hell I was talking about.

That's what I want you to think about when approaching a prospect. Never assume you understand what they need or want. To find out, you need to dig deeper and ask questions to understand what their opinions are about their situation, including what they've tried before to fix it and what they think they should do now. This is how you earn the right to offer a solution.

In "Chapter Four: Your Questioning Arsenal," I'll teach you different questioning strategies that will set you on a path to becoming a master at getting to the heart of a prospect's situation and their opinions around it. By doing so, not only will you be having a different conversation with your prospect than any of your competitors, but you'll also be helping the prospect clarify what they really need.

MINDSET MAKEOVER #3

Shed: Your prospect has all the authority and control.
Adopt: You have the same authority and control as your prospect.
This is known as equal business stature.

When you follow the prospect's system, the prospect has all the control. They can and do dictate the steps you must take to be included as a contestant, what information you must provide and the pricing and terms you must give in order to be considered. It reminds me of the scene from *Animal House* where the pledges are being hit by a paddle and must respond, "Thank you sir—may I have another?" It's humiliating and degrading and often doesn't get the prospect what they need.

I tell my clients, if you have a job and pay rent or a mortgage somewhere, you have the same authority and rights as your prospect. It begins with the simple stuff, like calling them by their first name. It's Bill and Melinda, not Mr. & Mrs. Gates. I know what some of you are thinking right now: "My mother always taught me to call people by Mr. and Mrs. It's respect!" Yeah, whatever. Your mom also taught you not to cross the street, not to talk to strangers and, for God's sake, don't talk about money! When someone calls me Mr. McKay in a business setting, I know I'm dealing with a chump. Your prospects know the same thing. I've also found that if someone corrects you for calling them by their first name, they're probably not going to be a very good prospect or client if you end up selling them something.

This equality between you and your prospect also means that you have every right (and responsibility) to disqualify prospects who aren't going to be the right fit. Yes, you have the right and obligation to tell them "No," if you determine they aren't yet ready for your solution or they're not willing to follow your sales process. You get to decide if your prospect will receive a proposal and when.

Equal business stature is a state of mind. You accept that you have it and act accordingly. It isn't arrogance, but rather a confidence that comes from having a full pipeline. Imagine if you had a meeting with a prospect who made it very clear that they were talking to five different vendors and that you must be the lowest price to win the business. Now imagine that you had nine other sales calls that week with deer prospects. How much time would you spend talking to your sales manager telling him that he needed to let you lower your price so you could compete for this deal? I would hope your answer would be "None."

Equal business stature means that you have the confidence to let your prospect know, up front, that you're qualifying them, as you know they're qualifying you. That, at the end of the meeting, you should both come to a yes-or-no decision (about something), and if it isn't a "Yes," then you are perfectly comfortable calling it a "No." It also means that, if you give something up to your prospect, it's normal and natural for you to get something from them in return. More on that in "Chapter Seven: The Close."

One of the main reasons we give the prospect all authority and power is because we are afraid—afraid because they have choices and can buy from someone else at the end of the day.

A friend shared a saying with me that seems to sum it up well—well enough that I adapted it as the title of my book:

Some will buy.

Some won't.

So what.

Who's next?

Meaning, "Who's the next prospect I need to be talking to?" Think of your clients in the same way.

MAINTAIN A HEALTHY PROSPECT PIPELINE

It's a fear common among salespeople—that a prospect will just buy from someone else if you don't give them what they want. When that fear arises, you might feel forced to cut your margins or give concessions to get the deal. Are you really forced to do these things? Or are you making excuses for a deeper problem?

I'm willing to bet that your real fear comes from knowing deep down that your prospecting pipeline sucks. If you had appointments set with 10 (or more) qualified prospects, and one started to give you trouble about pricing or terms or scope of work, how much time would you spend messing with them? I hope your answer is "As little as possible." The No BS Sales System will help you do that. And once you do, I want you to have enough control to say to a prospect, "I'm afraid I'm wasting your time. I don't think we're going to be the right fit for you." And then call on the next prospect.

I was having some drinks with a friend in the IT business one night. He looked terrible—tired, worried, overworked.

"Walker," he said. "My customers are driving me crazy." He then explained why.

He said they would call him, sometimes after hours or on weekends, and tell him they were having technical problems. He would drive over, diagnose the problem and tell them how much the part or software would cost. They would often tell him they could get the item on the internet for cheaper. So, he would either match their price or throw in the service for free.

"They don't understand that I'm not trying to rip them off. I'm just trying to give them the fix they need," he said.

"Why are you putting up with that shit?" I asked.

"What am I supposed to do? I don't want to lose my clients."

"Dude—you've lost control," I said. "You've trained them to treat you that way. They're treating you like their little bitch."

Now, I had his attention.

"The next time a client calls you after hours or on a weekend and asks you to fix something," I said, "ask them if it's important to get that fixed immediately or if they could wait until the next business day or two. Give them the option of waiting. Tell them, "I'll be happy to head over, but I'll have to bill you my after-hours rate, which is three times my normal rate.""

A look of relief washed over his face. "I can do that?" he said.

"Hell, yeah," I told him. "That's what business is. You have equal business stature. You're the same as them."

I wasn't suggesting he show his anger or act vindictively. I simply wanted him to assert his rights.

He needed to shift his mindset, and so do you. You need to reset the rules by changing your behavior. Negotiate upfront to manage expectations (yours and theirs) for not only each sales call but also for the business relationship afterwards. I'll tell you more about how to do that in "Chapter Two: The Necessary Preparations."

MINDSET MAKEOVER #4

Shed: I have to be the hero.
Adopt: I will be the guide.

In many stories, there's a "hero"—you know, the one at the beginning who faces a challenging problem he must solve. And sometimes there's a guide—the wise one who isn't the hero, but who shares sage advice to help the hero solve the problem. Think Luke Skywalker and Yoda.

A lot of people—but not you, of course—fall into the "hero trap" when they get into sales.

You know the hero trap, right? In order to feel good about yourself, you feel pressure to close every sale. When signs begin to show up that this one's not the right fit or just isn't going to close, the hero ignores the signs. The hero has to save everyone, right? He can't let one go, because he takes the rejection personally. If the hero can't close the sale, ring the bell, walk back into the office with a check, then, by his definition, he's a loser.

Everything is personal to the hero. That's the problem. It's all about him and satisfying his ego.

To avoid being the loser, the hero often pressures a prospect who isn't ready to make a change or tries to convince them they're making a horrible decision by not buying from him. This often ends when the hero begs and bargains and eventually gets pissed off and says he got screwed by the prospect, who wasted his time. When you behave like that, your prospect knows you don't have their best interests in mind. You get what's called "commission breath," and no amount of toothpaste or mouthwash will make it go away.

Great selling is never about you, the salesperson. Never.

It's always about the prospect.

REDEFINE VICTORY

Let's redefine victory in a sales call right here. Winning is getting a decision: yes or no. If it's not a "Yes," then it's a "No." Either one, prospect or salesperson, can call it over at any time. Simple. No pressure. No losers.

A guide gets to choose who they work with. If the client's expectations don't match up with what the guide can (and wants to) deliver, then the guide can say, "I'm not going to be the right fit," and that is certainly a victory!

Lose the ego—and the fear—and become a trusted guide for your prospect. Make your prospect feel like a hero for making the wise decision to hire you or not. Make your client feel like a hero for working with someone who understands their motivations, fears and desires better than anyone else who calls on them.

I go to Maine every summer for the first week of June to go trout fishing with several buddies. We fly-fish during the day and in the evenings drink liquor and laugh at old stories on our cabin's porch. It's one of my favorite weeks of the year.

During our first trip, years ago, we got assigned a guide named Gary. None of us knew a thing about fishing in Maine, but we were eager to learn. We met Gary at 9:30 on the first morning and set out to fish. He took us to a pond that he said was one of his favorites. Then he whipped out a little book he carried to keep track of how many fish his clients caught. "My average day is 57 fish caught in this pond," he said, making it sound like a bar we needed to meet.

At the pond, Gary showed us which fly to use and where to cast. If one of us missed a fish, Gary would say, "Damn, man, what's wrong with you?" He made it sound kind of funny, in a bros-in-a-boat kind of way.

If we landed a fish, he'd say, "See, I told you to cast there!"

For a while, it *was* kind of funny to have this crusty old Mainer helping us catch fish and giving us shit at the same time. He was the expert, right? And we were learning.

We fished for about four hours, ate some lunch and then got back in the boats to fish for the afternoon. I have to be honest: I like to trout fish, but I was looking forward to getting back and drinking bourbon on the porch. I asked him how long he normally fishes the pond, and he said, "The fish really start biting between 8:30 and 10 o'clock at night."

"Are you kidding?" I said. "That's hours from now. I'm kind of done for the day."

"But you'll miss the best fishing," he said.

"That's fine," one of my buddies said. "We don't want to fish that much."

"Aw, man, you guys are only at 37 fish. You're killing my daily average in this pond."

From that day on, every afternoon when we were ready to pack up our rods and head back to camp for happy hour, Gary would turn to his guiding partner and say with a dejected tone in his voice, "Rick, they want to go home. They don't wanna fish anymore. They're crushing my averages."

By the second night, we didn't care what he thought about how hard we wanted to fish. We were paying him. But the guilt-tripping got old. Gary was a guide who cared only about himself.

A couple of years later, we got hooked up with a new guide, Pete, who turned out to be the polar opposite of Gary. Pete showed up and said, "I've never fished with you guys before. Let's have a conversation. Tell me how long you like to fish. Are you hardcore fishermen, hoping to be catching fishing from sunup to sundown, or are you like some others I guide who like to fish, but if the fish aren't biting or the weather sucks, you'd just as soon be on the porch drinking liquor?"

"We're more like the second group. We're up here to relax. We like to fish, but we'd like to be back at camp by happy hour, around 4:30," I said.

"Great," Pete said. "We'll get you home by 4:30 for happy hour. One more question: Do you prefer fishing ponds or rivers?"

"What?" I said. "You mean there are rivers we can fish? Gary said there weren't any rivers worth fishing up here."

"That's probably because Gary hates fishing rivers. Man, there are great rivers up here we can fish if you'd like to do that."

We said we'd love to fish rivers this time.

Pete took us to a remote stretch of the Allagash River on the first day. It was beautiful water, and there were lots of holes and seams that held big native brook trout.

Like Gary, Pete suggested specific flies to use for each fishing spot. Unlike Gary, if we missed a fish, Pete would say, "Nice try. Let's give it another shot."

And if we caught a fish, he'd say, "Way to go!"

Pete was a true guide. The fishing and catching was never about him. It was about us, his clients. While we still laugh about fishing with Gary, the experience was completely different. Gary had to be the hero. Gary made it all about him and his wins and losses.

Even though we've been going to Maine for 20 years, we still hire Pete to guide us. Each year the waters change, the weather can be different and the patterns of flies change, too. We can count on Pete to help us. He knows where to fish and what the trout are eating. His intention is singular—to help us catch fish so that we have a great time—and he applies his considerable knowledge to achieve that goal.

I'm pretty certain that Pete appreciates us, too. We set clear expectations and show our appreciation and respect for him and his talents. And we don't bring any unnecessary drama or high-maintenance needs. It's a great fit for both of us.

In sales, you're looking for that great fit with your prospects and clients. Once you lose your ego, you can ask the right questions to make sure that a prospect is the right fit for you. Approaching as a guide, you can take the prospect through a sales process where they can disqualify themselves if they don't think you're the best fit for them. You're not wasting anyone's time. Even if you don't close a deal, you can move on easily because you know that there's another prospect out there who will need your help.

It may sound counterintuitive, but when going after prospects, I like hearing "No."

"Yes" is my favorite word, of course, but "No" comes in a very close second. I hear it all the time. I'd rather hear "No" now than after four or five sales calls, a bunch of presentations and a couple of high-dollar lunches.

A big part of the No BS Sales System is getting to "No" faster. Doing so helps you get to "Yes" faster and with prospects that are the right fit.

The hero complex can become apparent *after* a sale as well. I got my parents to switch financial advisors after Dad retired. My parents needed more handholding, and their current advisor wasn't set up well to do that for them. So, they switched and were very happy with the new advisor. I ran into him about six months after my parents had switched and told him how much I appreciated his help. He responded, "Thanks! We've got a great team." I'm sure he didn't mean it this way, but he sounded like an arrogant jerk. It would have been so easy and more appropriate to say, "We love having your parents as clients."

When you're in sales, it's never about you. Even after the sale.

CHAPTER ONE CHECKLIST

◆ Don't fall for the prospect's system. You might be if you're: doing most of the talking, not sure what's supposed to happen next, giving information without getting anything in return, and chasing someone who now has all of your info and isn't calling you back.

* Identify prospects that are ready, willing and able to make a change now (or in the near future). If they're not there yet, don't chase them. If they are "ideal" in every sense except for being ready, then keep them on your list, and reach out to them every 90 days or so.

* Identify the squirrels, deer and elephants in your current book of business and in your pipeline.
  * Cull your squirrels by raising prices to make room for better prospects.
  * Manage your elephants. Don't let them trample you!
  * Go after more deer.

* Focus your sales calls on learning your prospects' specific opinions about their current and future situations.

* Assume you have equal business stature with your prospects and clients. Behave as if you have the same rights and authority as them.

* Train your clients and prospects how to treat you with respect.

* Think like a guide. Sales is never about you.

* Work to understand what a prospect really wants and needs, and then be honest with yourself and them about your being the right person to help them. Congratulate them on their choice, whether they chose you or not. Let them be the hero!

❖　❖　❖

CHAPTER TWO

THE NECESSARY PREPARATIONS

U nderstanding the prospect's brain and adopting the key mindsets are only the start. Following the No BS Sales System requires a paradigm shift. You must think differently about both sales and people.

Take the critical step of pre-planning—coming up with a plan BEFORE you show up on your sales call. Creating a Pre-Call Plan is Step #1 in the No BS Sales System.

PRE-CALL PLAN

My buddy Jim was a pilot. Before he died far too early of pancreatic cancer, he flew almost 40 years and logged more than 10,000 hours of flying. I probably spent at least 400 hours in the plane with him over the last couple of decades. One of my favorite sayings of his was, "I'd rather be on the ground wishing I was in the air than in the air wishing I was on the ground." Jim was careful.

Before every flight, he called in to check the weather on the route. He filed a flight plan with the FAA, letting them know his route and destination. Before he took off, he went through a checklist to make sure all systems were working properly. As we taxied to the runway, Jim told me what he'd do if there were a stall during takeoff. "If we have enough air speed," he said, "I'll circle back to the airport. If not, there is a large, usually empty parking lot we'll put down in." His flying instructor had him practice both of those maneuvers every year.

Jim didn't like surprises and didn't want me to panic. I saw him go through this process many hundreds of times. I rode past the large (usually empty) parking lot on the way to the airport to see what we'd have to avoid if we ended up there! He told me 500 times what we'd do if the plane stalls.

Wanna guess how long 99% of sellers spend planning their sales calls before the meeting? Right. No time. If you ask about their plan, they'll look at you funny and say, "I'm gonna sell 'em. That's the plan." They're going to wing it. Would you want your heart surgeon to wing it? How about the pilot in control of your next flight? So why would you wing the next opportunity to make money for you and your family? Wing it, and you will almost guarantee your prospect will be in control. When that happens, you rarely win.

The first step of the No BS Sales System is planning your sales calls before you go. Preparation involves more than just gathering information about the other party. It also includes understanding your own goals and priorities, identifying potential obstacles and challenges and developing a plan for how to address them. By preparing thoroughly, you can enter the sales call with confidence and a clear sense of what you want to achieve. Arrive prepared, and it's much easier to follow the No BS Sales System and not the prospect's system.

Begin by asking yourself a series of questions to determine how to best approach your prospects and, more importantly, identify your weaknesses, and ditch them early on.

Question #1: Who are you meeting with and when?
I know what you're thinking: This is a dumb question. *If I already know who my prospect is, why would I need to ask myself this?* Don't think about this in the literal sense of simply knowing your prospect's name. Take note of their title or role in the company, for example, and ask yourself: Is this person in a position to make a decision for their company? Is this someone whose recommendation or information can help you move a sale forward? This is the first step in deciding what strategy you might employ in the call to get to the truth.

More initial things to think about: How do they dress? A big part of sales is making your prospect feel comfortable with you. Do you look like you belong there? In other words, do you look like a professional in your prospect's world? Are you meeting with an executive and need to wear a suit? Or are they more comfortable in jeans and boots?

I have a buddy who's a freelance writer. He once got an assignment to write in depth about a rodeo in California. He'd never covered rodeo cowboys, so he called the photographer who would accompany him for pointers.

"I know it sounds weird," the photographer said, "but dress like a cowboy."

"But that's not who I am," my buddy told him.

"Trust me on this," said the photographer. He had spent years shooting for *Sports Illustrated* and other magazines, but when he took his camera to his first rodeo, he couldn't connect with anyone. Only after he dressed the part did the cowboys let down their guard.

So my buddy put on cowboy boots, boot-cut Wranglers, a Western shirt and a cowboy hat, far from his normal khakis and button-up shirt. He didn't try to act like a cowboy, though. He introduced himself as who he was, a curious magazine writer who was a greenhorn when it came to rodeos. But that's all it took—honesty and a look that put the locals at ease.

No matter what you wear, make sure to wear decent clothes that fit well. You don't need expensive tailored suits. But finding a tailor—which can include the seamstress working at your mom-and-pop dry cleaner—who can help you improve your look is worth the effort and expense.

As much as how your prospects dress, consider their communication style. Are they more results driven or people driven? Do they get right to the point, or do they encourage some chitchat?

Question #2: How long will the meeting need to last?
You and your prospect should also agree on when you're meeting and, more important, how long the meeting will last.

Have you ever had a sales call where you knew you were going to need an hour, but after 20 minutes your prospect apologizes and says they have to leave for another meeting? Me, too. That sucks.

Part of being a successful communicator is having enough time to get your points across but also learning what you need to learn about your prospect's situation. Start by thinking through your time needs in advance. Do you need 10 minutes or two hours? Next, when you set up your meeting, make sure you ask for that amount of time.

When I set a meeting, I like to ask, "When would you have X amount of time to meet with me about Y?" I will often ask for a little longer than I think I'm going to need. Again, I tell them so. "It might not take that long," I'll say, "but if we're having a good conversation, I'd hate to cut it short."

This is part of setting proper expectations with your prospect. You don't want to throw them a curveball. If you don't manage their expectations about how long the meeting might take, they'll have their own expectations and might cut you off or end the meeting before you've covered what you need to cover.

DOUBLE-CHECK YOUR CALENDAR

Have you ever shown up for a meeting that you have in your calendar, but the prospect wasn't expecting you? Ugh. I have. I've also done the opposite, where I missed a meeting thinking it was at a different time because I didn't check. UGH! Reminder: Check the calendar and make sure that:

A) You've sent the meeting invitation.

B) They've accepted your invitation.

C) You're clear about whether this meeting is in person, over Zoom or by phone.

D) The date and time are clear and confirmed.

Question #3: Why does your prospect think you're meeting?

When my kids were young, they played soccer—not super-competitive soccer, but the kind where all the kids chase the ball around at the same time. I stood on the sidelines with the other parents, laughed and talked shit while our kids ran around. One of the dads, George, sold life insurance. He was super funny, and I usually hung out with him. We got to be buddies, and I looked forward to seeing him on Saturday mornings.

After a couple of months of hanging out at the soccer field, we decided to grab lunch. We talked about kids, sports, marriage, you name it. Just like on the soccer field, we enjoyed each other's company and laughed our asses off. A couple of weeks later, he invited me to lunch again, and I gladly went. Once again, we told stories and had fun. At the end of lunch, he grabbed the check, stood up and said, "So, what's it gonna take for the McKays to do business with me?"

I was completely taken off guard. Was that what this was all about? Him cozying up to me so he could sell me stuff? I think I stuttered something about already having a life-insurance guy that I work with whom I trusted but if something changed I'd let him know. (I've never had lunch with my agent before, by the way, and I'm fine with that. He's boring!)

After that, things were really awkward with George. He showed up at soccer the next week, and we waved, but we didn't hang out. I assume he was working on another mark to sell to.

If only he'd just said, "Hey, let's grab lunch again and talk business. I'm not sure if I could help you or even if you'd need my help, but I'd love to find out more about your financial plan and see if I could help you in some way. Would you be okay with that?"

"Sure," I probably would have said. Instead, the whole thing felt a little dirty, and I avoid the guy when I can—even 20 years later!

If you want your prospect to trust and respect you, let them know when you set the meeting what you want to talk about. If they say, "No, thanks," at least you know that and can cancel—or not set—the meeting. If they are open to it, they'll be prepared for the conversation. If they're surprised about why you're there, that's your fault for not setting clear expectations.

You can keep it as simple as, "Hey, would you grab a beer with me? I'd like to have a business conversation with you." Of course, it's even better if you provide more detailed information like the things you will talk about. For instance, you might say, "When we get together, do you mind if we figure out whether it makes sense to do X?" It all depends on the context, but here's the takeaway: Make sure both you and the prospect have a crystal-clear idea about why you're meeting.

DON'T FALL TO ZERO

I like this nugget of wisdom from FBI hostage negotiator Christopher Voss: "When the pressure is on, you don't rise to the occasion—you fall to your highest level of preparation."

Beware the inner voice telling you that going through these pre-planning steps is bullshit or that it will take too much time. Don't listen when that same false bravado says, "Man, I got this," when you don't. If you don't pre-plan for your sales calls, you'll fall to zero.

The No BS Sales System is a process. Pre-planning is a critical part of the process. Go through the steps, even if you've gone through them countless times before. That's how you get better.

Question #4: What's the best outcome you can expect from this meeting? (For me, it usually involves getting paid.)

When I was in the commercial real-estate business, I enjoyed working with buyers. Even though most commissions were paid by the seller at closing, I liked solving the myriad problems buyers faced before they could actually purchase a piece of property.

One of my friends owned a day spa and asked if I would help him find a second location. His original business was very successful, and he was ready to expand. I spent about a month looking at sites in the areas where he wanted to be. I showed him what I'd found, and we made an offer on the one he liked best. The seller accepted it, and then I went to work.

My client had never gone through the process of buying land to develop, so I told him I'd help him with the due diligence. I arranged the engineers, architects and lawyers and went to city hall to get plans approved. I put together packages for the different banks and helped him negotiate favorable financing for the project. I reached out to several contractors to get basic pricing for construction. We were able to get everything done in the 60 days we had requested and were moving toward closing the deal.

About a week before the deal was supposed to close—and I would have earned a $50,000 commission—the buyer called me in a panic. A national competitor, he said, was opening a location within a half a mile of his new site. He wasn't confident there was enough business for both of them, and he wanted out of the deal. So, we canceled it, and he walked away from the sale. The other professionals whom we hired—the engineers, architects, attorneys and consultants—got paid for their work, but because of the normal rules of the real-estate industry, I wasn't paid because no sale occurred.

Six months later, he called again to ask me to look for another site in a different part of town. He was confident that he could own the market over there and was ready to go. Just as before, I found a site, we put it under contract and I went to work. I brought in the same cast of characters to confirm the site was a good one and to get us numbers to build the new facility. Two weeks before closing, I got a call from him, once again in a panic, because he and his wife had decided to divorce and the timing of this was "just terrible." So, we killed the second deal, and I watched a $40,000 fee go up in smoke. Again, the professionals got paid.

These were not isolated events. This kind of thing happened all the time. I would show someone property for months, educate them on the market, help them solve different problems, and then they'd decide that maybe buying property was too risky. Other times my competitors would hear that a client was looking and would call them directly to show them property, and I would get cut out of the deal. Many of my good-faith efforts would lead me to not getting paid.

I had two epiphanies:

1. Maybe I was more committed to them buying a piece of property than they were. There are plenty of reasons not to buy a piece of real estate. If you look hard enough, you'll find something wrong with every piece of property and building in the world. The hardest part of my job was to find people who were committed to buy this imperfect product. Part of my role as broker was to help the buyer find those problems and decide whether or not to buy it anyway, but I was paid only if they actually did buy. It seemed to me my incentives were often misaligned with my client's.

2. People don't value things they don't pay for. Free information, no matter how much effort it took someone to put together, was worth exactly what someone paid for it. The lawyers, engineers and consultants got paid for the time they spent regardless if the deal closed. I wondered what jerk had made up the rule that real-estate brokers only get paid if and when a deal closes?

So, I decided to try something different. I was tired of working for free. I decided my *best outcome* would be to get paid for my "buyer service." I figured if someone wrote me a check for $5,000 to represent them, at least they had some skin in the game. If someone didn't think they needed my handholding or weren't committed to actually buying something, then I was okay walking away. I wasn't the right fit for everyone. That gave me a true differentiator.

Over the next month, I had four prospect meetings where I presented my new business model. All four people told me, "No, thanks." It felt weird to tell these people who said they were looking for new locations or investments that I wasn't going to be the right fit, but I was finished with free consulting.

I was referred to a doctor who wanted to buy a building for his practice. I told him I'd be happy to meet with him but that I worked differently from other brokers and that we should talk to make sure I was going to be the right fit for him.

We met, and I asked him why he thought he needed help buying a new building. He said, "I operate on brains. I've got decades of experience doing that. I've never bought a building before, and I want someone to advise me, so I don't make a stupid mistake."

I told him I could help him, but I charged $5,000 upfront. This would allow me to help him find the right location, help him with due diligence, and if I found a reason that he shouldn't buy it, I could tell him so with no hesitation. If he did buy something, however, the seller would pay my fee.

He said, "I had no idea a service like that existed. That is awesome." He wrote me a check for $5,000, and, 90 days later, he was closing on an office building we'd found off market. I collected a $41,000 fee at closing on top of my $5,000 retainer.

Two weeks after the doctor closed on his new building, he referred me to his wealth advisor. The wealth advisor said he had two clients who needed help finding investment property, but he didn't have anyone he trusted to help them. When he heard about my model, he was intrigued. He said it was great to find someone in the real-estate business whose incentives were aligned with the client's. Soon after we met, he introduced me to his clients, who wrote me a check for $5,000 during our first meeting.

Four months later, they bought an apartment complex, and I earned another $57,000 commission.

The referrals kept coming.

START WITH A MONKEY'S FIST

A monkey's fist is a knot used during the age when large sailing ships were the norm for travel and commerce. The ropes sailors used for rigging the sails and securing boats to piers or other boats at sea were too heavy and hard to throw. So, sailors used a smaller rope to tie a ball-shaped knot—the monkey's fist—around a lead weight to give it some heft and make it easier to throw. Sailors attached this knot to a length of narrow cord, and they tied the other end of the cord to the heavy rope. Then they threw the monkey's fist across the water to a crew on a pier or second ship. The crew caught the weighted knot and hauled on the cord until the rope end reached them.

You're probably asking, "What the hell does this have to do with sales?"

A lot.

If you're in the business of selling something expensive and complicated—something custom, where you might find yourself doing a bunch of free consulting for people who end up not buying—you need to first sell a monkey's fist. Think of it as selling something small before you sell something big. What's something you currently do for free for prospects? Is it a survey, evaluation, deep dive, audit, overview or assessment? Instead of giving that information away for free, call that the first step of your process and charge for it. Think of it as getting paid for your proposal.

I know what you're thinking: "No one would pay me for that. All of my competitors do that for free." That's exactly why you should charge for it. If you knew you were getting paid to do that work, how much more in depth could you go? Might you also feel better about telling your prospect "No" if, during your due diligence, you figure out you aren't going to be the right fit? If someone pays you to do this work, how many other proposals do you think they get? When you call a plumber, and he charges $150 to come to your house to diagnose the problem, how many plumbers do you call?

Chances are you're going to get a fair number of "No's," especially at first. But think about it: If your prospect isn't committed enough to spend a little bit of money with you to help them figure out their problem, what do you think your chances are of getting them to actually buy from you after they've talked to two others and are now spreadsheeting your pricing?

The funniest thing to me was that the people who said, "This will never work as a business model" were my competitors. They'd ask, "Why would someone pay you for what I'd do for free?" I'd just smile and say, "I'll be happy to refer you to the ones who won't pay me."

The guy who owned the day spa called me back several months later and said he was ready to go buy something now. I told him about my new business model, and he said, "Thanks, but no thanks." He ended up working with another broker friend of mine, who didn't charge him anything. Five years later, after multiple failed attempts, the day-spa operator bought a second location. I was happy for him, but I was also glad I'd let someone else chase that deal.

Why share that story here? To encourage you to both think big and make it happen. Asking yourself, *"What's the ideal outcome you can expect from this meeting?"* forces you to get real—to set clear and specific expectations for you and your prospect.

Most of the time, our sales cycle is long because we, the sellers, *make* it long. We can't imagine someone buying in one meeting, so we unwittingly make it so they can't. We assume it's going to take multiple meetings, and don't ask for any decisions other than, "Hey, can we meet again?"

I guess it's a good way to push off hearing "No" as long as you can. But that sounds like a loser's strategy to me.

Think of it this way: If someone has pain now that they're committed to fixing, has the authority to fix it and trusts you completely, how many meetings would you make them go through to hire you?

One? Two? More than two?

Come on. If someone can meet with a neurosurgeon one time for 30 minutes and decide to let her operate on their brain, how many meetings are you going to make a prospect sit through to buy your software or your forklift or hire you to manage their money?

What's your best outcome?

* Payment and a signed contract?
* A purchase order?
* A non-refundable down payment or retainer?

I know what you're thinking: *Walker, that isn't how **my** business works. Nobody does that.*

That's the point.

To get what no one else is getting, you have to do what no one else is doing.

Also, and you know this already, until money changes hands, you have *nothing*.

But, Walker, we've got to learn way more stuff than we can get in one meeting to see if they'd be a fit for us.

I had a custom homebuilder argue with me about this. He said, "We've got to create a bid for each homeowner and then go over it to make sure they understand it." He will often then go back and value-engineer the project to get it to a number his prospect can stomach. He said it often takes multiple people multiple days to get the information ready for the prospect.

"What percentage of those do you close?" I asked him.

He looked at the floor and said, "Maybe 20 percent."

"Why so low?" I asked.

"Most people have no idea how much a new home like they want costs, so they call me and ask me to work up a bid to see if their fantasy can become a reality." More than half of his prospects simply gasp at the cost and never call him back.

He now charges $7,500 to do a bid and closes 80% of people who hire him. The funny part, he said, is that he's getting more referrals now than ever and his reputation as expensive and trustworthy is a great differentiator. He says he can now afford to spend more time on each project to make sure he's delivering what his clients want.

Think about it. What's something now that you're probably giving for free that is valuable information?

Maybe your best outcome is having your prospects pay you something significant to engage you to do that study for them.

Question #5: What's a good-but-not-perfect outcome?
If your prospect can't accept a "Yes" or "No" to your ideal outcome, what's your backup plan? What's another way to get them to demonstrate commitment—to put some skin in the game? If they don't have the authority to write a check, maybe you get them to decide whether to introduce you to the person who does. Or maybe it's simply that you discover a specific problem worth following up on. Whatever the case, in your mind—and on paper—set the expectation that, at the end of the meeting, you and your prospect will come to a yes-or-no agreement on taking a pre-agreed-upon concrete step, one that moves you closer to achieving your best outcome.

As with any good negotiation, know your limits before the meeting starts. Have a concrete idea of the minimum thing that you're willing to accept, and get ready to let them know about it. If they ask you to send the information through email or ask for more stuff for free, think about whether it's worth doing that or if you'd simply prefer to hear a "No" from the get-go. That way, you're not wasting each other's time.

Question #6: What questioning strategies will you use to better understand their situation?

Have you ever walked out of a sales call and thought, *Damn, I forgot to ask that question!* Use this section to remind yourself about the specific questioning strategies (that you'll learn about in "Chapter Four: Your Questioning Arsenal"). A bunch of my clients have told me how helpful it was to remind themselves about the questioning tools they have *before* they go to the meeting. We're a little ahead of ourselves here. You're smart, so I'm not worried about getting ahead. This is the time to remind yourself about the questions you've got at your disposal that will get you data, of course, but also will solicit your prospect's opinions about the data. Here's a taste of some of the questioning strategies you'll learn in Chapter Four.

- ❖ "Good/Bad" questions: Use these to figure out what's important to your prospect and how strong the incumbent's position is.

- ❖ "Let's pretend" questions: These will help you get your prospect to share their opinions about something that might happen in the future. Think of it like a trial balloon. "Let's pretend it's a year from now, but you hired us today. What would have to happen in the next 12 months for you to be able to say, 'Hiring you was a great choice. I'm so glad we did that.'"

◆ "Reversing" questions: Instead of answering a question with a response, ask a clarifying question instead. "I appreciate you asking about product color. Tell me why that's important to you right now."

◆ "Third-party" stories: Instead of sharing your own opinions (no one cares what you think), tell them what other people think. "Our top clients tell us that our customer service is the best they've ever experienced."

◆ "Assumptive" questions: Use these to let people know what you do without actually telling them. "When your financial advisor visits with you once a quarter, goes over your statements and asks about any changes in your life or goals so they can make sure your investment risk profile hasn't changed, what kind of things did y'all talk about last quarter?"

◆ "Columbo" questions: This strategy involves playing "dumb" to get your prospect to elaborate or open up with more information. "You said you wouldn't spend more than $5,000 to fix this problem. Mind if I ask where that number came from?"

TALKING POINTS: KNOW YOUR PROSPECT'S DISC PROFILE

How much do you know about DISC profiles? A century ago, an American psychologist, William Moulton Marston, developed the theory that led to this popular behavioral-assessment tool. (And check this out: He also invented an early prototype of the lie-detector test and was a cartoonist who created the character of Wonder Woman, based on the polyamorous life partner he shared with his wife.)

I bring the DISC assessment up here because understanding a prospect's communication style can help you understand them and give you tools to make them more comfortable with you.

The four main communication styles are: Dominance (D), Influence (I), Steadiness (S) and Conscientiousness (C).

Here's my unprofessional, highly opinionated short take on the four types:

◆ People with a Dominant (D) communication style are typically results-driven, assertive and confident. They like to win. When selling to a D, it's important to be direct, confident and focused on the end result. Avoid small talk, and get straight to the point. Being skeptical that a D really needs your help can be an effective tactic in getting to the truth quickly.

◆ People with an Influencer (I) communication style are typically outgoing, charismatic and enjoy socializing. When selling to an I, it's important to build rapport and establish a personal connection. After they're comfortable, make sure to establish the rules for the meeting so you don't end up playing "Who do you know?" for the rest of the sales call. Use third-party stories about why other people like them decided to make the purchase. A big win for an I is to solve a problem that's been making people unhappy. Don't confuse their fun-loving nature and friendliness with their willingness to buy.

◆ Prospects with a Steady (S) communication style are typically calm, patient and reliable. They typically don't like change. These people have had the same three best friends since fourth grade. When selling to an S, it's important to build trust and establish a long-term relationship. They won't want to ruffle any feathers, so if your product or service means big change, it's going to be a tough sell. Human Resources is usually full of S's. S's also often have "resting bitch face," so it's hard to know where you stand.

◆ Prospects who communicate in a Conscientious or Cautious style (C) are typically detail-oriented, analytical and precise. When selling to a C, it's important to provide detailed information and data to support your claims. You can't give them enough data. C's are desperately afraid of making a mistake and want to cover their butt. All the charm in the world won't help you sell to a C. C's don't want any surprises, so be sure to manage their expectations (and yours) during the sales process.

There are AI-powered personality assessment tools such as Crystal Knows or Crystal for LinkedIn, which analyze a person's writing style and social-media presence to predict what their DISC profile/communication style will be. However, it's important to note that these tools are not always accurate and should be used as a supplement to other indicators.

Question #7: Where could you screw this up?
This question takes some self-reflection. What could you do, or what could you miss that could keep you from getting to the truth with your prospect? Famous investor Charlie Munger, Warren Buffet's closest partner, had a favorite saying: "Invert, always invert." What he meant by that was to think about what you don't want to happen and go backwards from there. By doing so, you can come up with a plan to make sure that the bad outcome won't happen. While you can't control what decision the prospect may make about buying your product or service, you can control what you do. Think about the last time you walked out of a meeting and gave yourself a Homer Simpson "Doh!" because you forgot to ask a question or didn't ask the prospect about their decision-making process. Take that feeling, and use it to make sure you don't screw that up again.

You have nothing in sales until you have a check in your hand. You have nothing to lose. Take a minute, and think about what you might do or not do that would cause you not to win.

- If I don't manage my prospect's expectations.
- If I fail to uncover and address an unspoken objection by my prospect.
- If I don't ask about their budget.
- If I fail to follow the No BS Sales System and fall prey to the prospect's system.
- If I fall for a positive prospect.

People make changes because they have pain. By identifying the things you screwed up in the last sales call that now cause you pain, you'll probably have a good list of things to avoid this time.

Question #8: What are your biggest fears about this meeting or prospect?
The previous question involved thinking about how you might screw up the call. This question is about smoking out any objections or hesitations your prospect might have **in advance** and before you get too far in your sales cycle**.** If there's a common objection or issue that's come up more than once in the past (either with this prospect or one like them), let's name it here. I'll show you in the next chapter how to deal with it at the beginning of the sales call. No reason to waste your prospect's time if you know upfront reasons they won't buy from you.

Here are some examples of biggest fears:

◆ My biggest fear is that you're meeting with me because you're nice, not because you have any reason to make a change.

◆ My biggest fear is that you're hoping what I have will be cheaper than what you're paying now.

◆ My biggest fear is that you're going to like what we have but won't have the budget to pay for it.

◆ My biggest fear is that we'll get to the end of this meeting, and, even though you'll be thinking, "Nope, this isn't the right fit," you'll say something like, "Let me think it over" or "Why don't you call me in a week?" If that's where we are at that point, do you mind if we just call it a "No"?

If there's going to be a problem, when do you want to know? Me? As soon as possible!

In the next chapter, I'll show you how to voice those and other fears with your prospects in an honest and non-confrontational way that will save you time and hassle.

CHAPTER TWO CHECKLIST

Before your next sales call, pre-plan using the eight questions:

1. *Who are you meeting with and when?*

2. *How long will the meeting need to last?*

3. *Why does your prospect think you're meeting?*

4. *What's the best outcome you can expect from this meeting?*

5. *What's a good but not perfect outcome?*

6. *What questioning strategies will you use to better understand their situation?*

7. *Where could you screw this up?*

8. *What are your biggest fears about this meeting or prospect?*

❖ ❖ ❖

CHAPTER THREE

REWRITING THE RULES

When I was a kid, I had a dentist who was probably a nice guy, but I freaking hated him and hated going to see him. I realized much later in life that it was because I never knew what was going to happen when I entered that chamber of horrors! He was either going to use that awful-tasting, fluoride toothpaste, jab a needle into my gums or fire up that whining drill and bury it into a tooth. I dreaded those visits and the dark uncertainty that awaited me. Once I got older, moved into my own place and started making my own decisions, I didn't go to the dentist for a while.

Then I got married, and my wife, reminding me that going to the dentist is necessary, convinced me to try again. She sent me to her dentist, Dr. Julia, and I noticed a difference immediately.

I walked through the door, and the receptionist greeted me and made me feel welcome. Dr. Julia came out and said, "Walker, you're going to be with us for about 30 minutes. The hygienist will clean your teeth, and then we'll take some X-rays. After that, I'll come back, and we'll have a five-or-ten-minute consultation about what I see. If anything needs to be corrected, you can decide what you want done and when you want to schedule it. We'll talk about cost and anything else you have questions about. Is that going to be okay with you?"

"That all sounds fine," I said.

"And by the way, what flavor of toothpaste do you want? We have four varieties."

I thought, *Holy shit—this is great.*

I learned a lot from Dr. Julia that day—not only what good dental care looks like but also how important it is to manage people's expectations.

For some, meeting with a salesperson can feel a lot like going to a dentist, minus the needles and drills. If you don't know what to expect, it can be scary. As a professional salesperson, you have the power to take the scary stuff away. How? Be transparent with prospects. Let them know what's going to happen. Show them that you have a process. Build trust with them.

In sales, unless you negotiate different rules, you'll often find yourself following a prospect's unspoken rules. As you know from earlier chapters, those rules—the prospect's system—are rarely in our favor. The No BS Sales System balances the scales and replaces the prospect's one-sided system. And there's no trickery. You get to be completely transparent about it.

In the old sales system, the only acceptable answer your prospect could give was "Yes," as in "Yes, I want to buy it." But "Yes" may not be the right answer for your prospect or you! By following the No BS Sales System, both you and your prospect have permission to say "Yes" or to say "No" to taking the next step. Either one is completely okay. If it's going to be a "No," though, you want to learn that as soon as possible. Remember, you're not the right fit for everyone. If it's going to be a "No," let's learn about it ASAP. In sales, your ability to make money is based on two things: your time and the information you gather. If you don't put a high value on both by being willing to walk away, you can bet your prospect won't, either.

TALKING POINTS: DON'T SOUND LIKE A JACKASS

I want you to ban the words "my time" from your vocabulary forever, as in "my time is valuable" or "I don't want to waste my time." Whenever the words "my time" come out of your mouth in a sales situation, you sound like a jackass. Whenever you're about to say, "My time," I want you to catch yourself and say, "Your time." It means the same thing, but since sales is *never* about you, don't make this about you, either.

Instead of *saying,* "My time is valuable," *show it* by putting a value on that time. Remember my commercial real-estate example, where I charged people $5,000 up front to work with them? Here's the way I looked at it: If somebody wasn't willing to spend $5,000 with me to represent them in the marketplace, then they clearly didn't value what I was offering—my time and my experience. They didn't have pain around that. I wasn't angry. I knew I wasn't the right fit for everyone. That was their choice, and they had other options.

The second step of the No BS Sales System is to level the playing field between you and the prospect—to create equal business stature. No games: All rules are discussed and agreed upon before you start. Your transparency will be one of your differentiators from your competition.

ESTABLISH THE RULES

You may have played side-yard football as a kid. There was a kid in my neighborhood whose parents had a vacant lot next to their house. We treated it as the neighborhood football field and played there after school all the time.

When someone new came to play, even before we divided into teams, we would establish the rules: whether it was two-hand tag or tackle, how we scored points, the locations of the goal line and sidelines. If someone didn't like the rules, they could suggest different ones—or decide not to play the game.

Would you play a game with big stakes if your opponent knew the rules—but you didn't? Or would you play a game with big stakes where you knew the rules—but those rules drastically limited your chance of winning? That's like buying lottery tickets—a fun distraction but a horrible way to run your business. If you follow the prospect's process in sales, you're gambling not only with your money but also your time.

When you follow the No BS Sales System, you negotiate the rules up front. And if you don't like the rules that your prospect demands, you don't have to play. The same goes for your prospect. If they don't like the rules that you want, they can say, "No, thanks" as well. All the pressure is taken off of both you and the prospect up front because there will be no surprises.

Robert Cialdini, in his book *Influence: The Psychology of Persuasion*, talks about the Law of Reciprocity. This law says that if you do something for someone else, they will be more inclined to do something for you. This is especially true if you ask for what you want before doing the thing for them. "I'll be happy to drive, if you'll pay for gas," or "I'll pay for lunch today, if you get the next one." In the context of sales: "If I'm okay coming over there to meet with you, will you be okay getting the other key stakeholders into the room so we can make a decision?"

You can't get angry at people for not doing what they didn't know they were expected to do.

You must be willing to ask for what you need, be that a decision, information, access, money or something else in return for what the prospect asks of you.

Here's an example of getting something in return: When making a prospecting call, ask, "Do you mind if I take 30 seconds to tell you why I called, and then you can decide whether or not we should keep talking?" In other words, *I'll give you the right to hang up if you'll give me 30 seconds to give my pitch.* The prospect feels like she is in control, and you get what you want. Everyone's expectations are managed.

UNCLEAR IS UNKIND (AND POTENTIALLY EMBARRASSING)

During my early days in the commercial real-estate business, I listed a building for sale that was owned and occupied by a general contractor. Hell, I was so green, I'm not even sure I knew what a contractor was. But I had learned that, if a building was suitable for one contractor, it might be suitable for another. So, I started calling contractors.

This building was 20 miles west of the city in what was a tiny rural community called Red Bank. I knew that building wasn't going to sell itself, so I looked up contractors in the yellow pages and started dialing, beginning with AAA Contractors. I was prepared to go alphabetically till I got to the end of the Z's. I paid no attention to their current location and had no clue about their size. I just put my head down and called. After a couple of hours of dialing (and getting no response), I'd gotten deep into the B's. Next on the list was Bradley Plumbing. I almost fell out of my chair when I got Mr. Bradley on the phone. I quickly introduced myself and said, "I've got this building out in Red Bank. I'd love for you to come look at it."

"Sounds great," he said, and we chose a place to meet. I was thrilled that I finally had a prospect for the building!

We met at a crappy little shopping center in a place called Three Fountains, about seven miles east of the building.

"You want to get in my car or take your truck?" I asked.

"Let's take my truck," he said.

We were riding along having a great conversation. After a few miles, I handed him one of my sales brochures.

He looked at me kind of funny and threw the brochure on his Styrofoam-covered dash. "Uh, tell me about the building," he said. "How's the plumbing?"

"Oh, it's fine," I told him. "In really good shape."

"Okay," he said, sounding confused, "then why the hell did you call me?"

"I was hoping you'd buy the building," I said, now realizing I had a problem.

"Wait. What? Oh, hell no! Who would want to own a building way the f*ck out here?"

He turned the truck around and began one of the longest 10-minute rides of my life back to the strip center where I'd left my car. He was mad at me, and I was mad at him. Neither of us spoke the whole way back. I'm not even sure we said goodbye!

The moral of this story? Be clear about what you want. Be sure your prospect knows what you want. And manage those expectations before you meet. Being clear is kind. Being unclear is the opposite, regardless of your intentions.

SETTING AN OPENING AGREEMENT

The best way to set clear expectations with a prospect before your sales call officially begins is with an Opening Agreement. You'll want to discuss the following: how much time needs to be allotted for the meeting, what you both want to talk about, that "No" is an okay answer for either of you and what "Yes" would mean if it's the right fit. Any obvious objections need to be brought up before they come up. In short, you need to confirm the time, agenda, decision and your biggest fear. Here's a handy acronym to help you remember it: TADB, pronounced "TAD-Buh." It rolls off the tongue, like NASA or RADAR, right? Okay, so as an acronym, it sucks. But I bet you won't forget it. Say it: TAD-buh. (Kinda catchy, right?)

While the eight questions in the pre-call plan from the previous chapter help you prepare for sales calls, creating an opening agreement using TADB will help both you and your prospect manage expectations when you get together to talk business.

TIME

Start by asking, "How much time did you set aside for this meeting today?" You'll show your prospect that you respect his time. Plus, if he's thinking 10 minutes and you were hoping for an hour, you'll want to know that ASAP. By the way, if this I've-only-got-10-minutes scenario happens, it doesn't mean you need to talk fast. Use the 10 minutes to set another meeting when the prospect does have the hour that you need.

The best time to set expectations is when you first schedule the meeting. If you're going to need an hour, ask them to pick a time to meet when they'll have an hour. When you do get together, confirm the time they have allotted, in case things have changed.

AGENDA

There are two parts to this. First, you want to know what they want to learn from you during this meeting. Next, you want to get permission to ask questions as well. It's kind of fun to watch people's expressions when you ask them first what they want to talk about. They usually don't expect that question from a salesperson, and it often shows on their face. It's a pattern interrupt.

A great way to ask about their agenda is to pose it as a "Let's pretend" question. That might sound like, "Let's pretend it's the end of the meeting and you're saying to yourself, 'This has been a great meeting. I learned exactly what I wanted to learn.' What would we have covered to make you be able to say that?" You want to know what's on their mind or what they want to learn. Often the things they'll want to talk about are the problems they've got now and maybe what you can do to fix them.

When they share the things they want to cover, take notes. Show them you paid attention. You might even repeat it back to them. You might say, for example: "Okay, so you said you want to talk about your cash flow and your location and your receivables. We'll certainly cover that."

This doesn't necessarily mean you're going to cover and address all that during the first meeting. You're in charge of what you share and when, and it might not be advantageous to you to share everything today. Acknowledging that you heard them by repeating it back and assuring them you'll cover it lets them know you're in tune with them.

I know what you're thinking: What if they say, "I don't know. You're the one who wanted to meet." First of all, don't get defensive. This is not a big deal. You can respond with, "That makes sense. I did ask for the meeting. I do value your time, however, and if there is something you'd like to know from a guy who spends a lot of time living in and thinking about _____ (your space), please let me know. I don't want to waste your time."

When I was young in the commercial real-estate business, I'd occasionally ask a question that would cause my prospect to respond with, "That's none of your business!" These questions often revolved around money or other emotional issues. At first,

I internalized that it wasn't my business to know personal details, so I quit asking about them. Later I learned that it *literally was* my business to know how people felt about problems they were having around money and other things. Like when your doctor asks permission before they touch and examine one of your body parts, we need to get permission to ask about what we need to examine in our conversation.

In a nutshell, I want permission to ask about a prospect's pain, their budget and their decision-making process. Now, pain is a buzzword in sales, and I don't like using that word with prospects. Yes, I want to know their pain, but I don't want to label it as such. Instead, I'll ask for permission to discuss a contrast between where they are and where they want to be.

For example, after the prospect has shared what they want to learn from me, I'll proceed to the second part of the "agenda" by saying, "I've got some things I'd like to learn from you as well. Are you okay if I lay them out so we can be completely transparent with each other?

"Sure," is the typical response. (I've never had anyone tell me "No" when I asked to share my agenda.) Then I proceed with: "Thanks, I appreciate that. I'd like your permission to ask you about your current situation, what's working and maybe what's not. I want to find out how much money you're currently spending on X and explore where you could find more if you needed it. And if it does make sense to make a change, I'd like to find out how you make decisions around here. Will you be okay if we talk about those things?"

I'm sure you picked up that I just asked permission to ask about their pain, their budget and their decision-making process.

This does two things. One, by asking permission, you're giving your prospect a heads-up that you do have a plan. You're not just winging it. Next, if your prospect isn't comfortable talking about one of those three things—each of which you'll need to know to see if they're the right fit—let's learn that now! My experience has shown me that if I get permission first, I can ask almost anyone about anything.

DECISION

What should the title be of every person you have a sales call with?

Decision maker.

What's their job?

To make decisions.

Now that we've established that, I want you to believe that every sales call should end with a decision. Either a "Yes" to a predetermined next step or a "No," meaning you're not going to move forward now. You'll want to make it explicitly clear that both "No" and "Yes" are good answers and that, if both of you aren't sure moving forward is the right step, you're going to agree to call it a "No," with no hard feelings. Once again, this transparency will set you apart from your competitors. It's important to remember that you're not going to ask for a "Yes" at the end of the meeting, but for a decision.

So, let's break this down. First you ask permission to tell them "No." Then, you give them permission to tell you "No" in return. Next, establish that "Yes" is also a possible outcome, and then define what steps must happen if you both agree that it's a "Yes." Easy-peasy, right?

Here's what it sounds like: "Great, thanks. I need to ask you a favor. If I get the feeling that we're not going to be the right fit, do you mind if I just tell you so?"

This is another WTF moment for your prospect in the sales call. A *salesperson* asking permission to tell the *prospect* "No"? You just told your prospect that you might disqualify them. That is different! Most of your prospects will visibly relax a little and say something like, "Yeah, I'd appreciate that."

Now, let's give something in return: "Would you mind doing the same for me? If you're not completely comfortable that taking a next step is the right choice for you, would you just tell me "No?" I promise I won't try to change your mind."

This is really wild. You just gave your prospect permission to tell you "No." That may feel like some scary shit to you, but they already know they can tell you "No." You're just asking for an explicit "No" if that's what they're thinking. If they're not going to buy, when do you want to know? (Me? ASAP!) Many of your prospects will quickly and proudly tell you, "Absolutely. I can definitely tell you 'No.'"

So now we've established a timeline for the meeting. We've each told the other what we want to talk about. And we've given each other permission to say "No" if we don't think moving forward is the right move. Next, we need to establish that "Yes" is also a possibility and what "Yes" would mean.

Remember that pre-call plan you did before this sales call? You wrote down what an ideal outcome for this sales call would look like. Here's where that pre-work comes in handy. Now it's time to come to an agreement about what the next step would be if we did agree to move forward. Might as well start with proposing your ideal outcome.

Let's say your ideal outcome was for the prospect to sign a contract and give you a deposit. Here's how you ask for that: "Typically, at the end of a meeting like this, we're deciding whether or not it makes sense for you to sign a contract and give us a deposit to get started. Would you be okay making that decision at the end of the meeting?"

There are a couple possible outcomes here. One, they could say "Sure," and then you confirm it by saying, "Great. Anything less than your thinking it's a great idea to sign the contract and give us a deposit, then we can call it a 'No.' Are you okay with that?"

The other response they could give you when you're asking for your ideal outcome is, "Well, no, I'm not prepared to decide whether or not to sign a contract and give you a deposit." Okay, that's fine, too. Here's where your pre-call plan will help you again: Now you suggest your okay-but-not-ideal outcome.

Let's say your okay-but-not-ideal outcome was to set another meeting with other decision-makers. Here's how that goes: "Hey, that makes sense. What if we decide at the end of the meeting whether or not it makes sense to schedule another meeting with other decision-makers who need to be a part of this process. Would you be okay if we decide that today?"

If they're okay with that, then, once again, summarize it to make sure everyone understands. "Okay, perfect. At the end of the meeting, anything less than you being completely comfortable that setting another meeting between me and your other colleagues is a great idea, let's call it a 'No.'"

I know what you're thinking: *Sometimes I might meet with someone who's been charged with gathering information, whose job it is to report the findings to a board or another person who will make the final decision.* They can't tell me "Yes" or "No." I get it. That happens fairly frequently. In those situations, however, the decision-maker is most likely going to ask the information gatherer which option they recommend. If they don't recommend your option, the chances of you getting picked are very low. So here's your ideal outcome for that situation: "Let's do this: At the end of this meeting, can you tell me whether or not you can endorse my solution to the board? If you're not 100% comfortable with endorsing my stuff, we can call it a 'No.' Are you okay with that?"

A couple of things here. If they aren't okay saying "Yes" or "No" to your good-but-not-ideal suggestion, you can then ask them what they'd like to decide today. To stay out of the prospect's process, you must have transparency. It's my experience that, if the prospect pushes back here and doesn't want to agree on any decision for an outcome, you're wasting time. It doesn't mean they're bad people; it just means they're not ready. It's okay to end the call here and move on.

Second, help them remember that, if they're not comfortable, they can simply tell you "No" as well. If you think about it, you're giving them something they already know that they can do! Make it known that you're okay with hearing a "No" and that you won't chase them down the street or wrestle with them further for approval. Not only does this set expectations, but it also tends to put the prospect at ease when working with you.

It's a mental game changer when you ask for your ideal outcome the first time and your prospect says, "Sure, I can make that decision." Here's a warning though: After the second time someone says "Yes" at the end of the meeting to your ideal outcome, you'll be mad as hell at yourself for ever asking for or accepting less than that again. Your ideal outcome might become your new "Okay-but-not-ideal" outcome.

The bottom line is, your meetings should be about making decisions, getting "Yes's" and "No's." If a prospect knows at the beginning of the meeting what decision she needs to make, it will help her focus on the things that she'll need to know to make that decision. You, having a clear agenda as well, can focus on what you need to know to do the same.

BIGGEST FEAR

Remember during our pre-planning, when I asked you to list things that could go wrong? Here is where you can share those things with your prospect. Think of it like dealing with objections before they come up.

COMMON OBJECTIONS

If you've been in sales for even a minute, chances are you already have experience with prospects raising objections to what you're offering. Based on your previous interactions, what objections are likely to come up? More importantly, what objections could kill the deal even if you resort to your backup plan? Be aware also of unspoken objections indirectly communicated by your prospect. You don't want to realize too late that they were actually trying to say "No." Here are examples of possible objections:

- They don't have the money.

- They're looking for a supplier or service provider who's cheaper, and you're not it.

- They're already working with somebody else, who they will have a tough time firing to hire you.

- They think your business is too small for you to adequately look after them.

- Your business is so big they fear being neglected.

TADB ROLE PLAY

Using TADB, here's how the back-and-forth might go between you and a prospect while negotiating an opening agreement.

TIME

(Confirming the time allotted for the meeting.)

You: How much time did you set aside for this meeting?

Prospect: You told me to expect an hour, so I have an hour.

You: Perfect. Do you have a hard stop in an hour, or is it okay if we run over a bit because we both agree it's worth spending some extra time?

Prospect: No. No hard stop, but I do have a lot to do today.

You: I get it. I'll keep a close eye on the time and make sure we don't run over unless we both agree to do so.

Prospect: Thanks

AGENDA

(What is theirs? What is yours?)

You: Let's pretend it's the end of the hour. We're finishing up here, and you're telling me we covered exactly what you wanted to cover today. What would we have talked about in this next 60 minutes for you to be able to say that?

Prospect: Well, I would like you to tell me about A, B and C.

You: Okay, great. You want me to cover A, B and C. We will definitely go over that. Anything else?

Prospect: Nope. Those things are plenty.

You: Great. I have some things I would like to ask you about as well. Do you mind if I share those things with you?

Prospect: Sure.

You: Okay, cool. I want to ask you about your current situation—what you like and maybe what you wish were better or different. Also, I want to find out about your budget (or how much money you are currently spending on _____), and I would like to ask you about how, if you wanted to make a change, you would go about doing that? Are you okay if I ask you about that stuff?

Prospect: Sure.

DECISION

(You can say "No." They can say "No." Confirm what "Yes" would look like.)

You: May I ask you a favor?

Prospect: Sure.

You: If I get the feeling at any time that our service/product isn't the right fit for you, do
you mind if I am straight with you and tell you so?

Prospect: Sure! That would be great.

You: Good. Thanks. Do you mind doing the same for me? If, at any point in our conversation, you get the feeling that we aren't the right fit for you, do you mind telling me that?

Prospect: Sure!

You: I promise if you feel that way, I won't try to change your mind.

Prospect: Great.

You: Here's a harder question: Let's pretend we get to the end of our conversation, and you're thinking, "I'm comfortable moving forward!" and I am thinking "I think this makes sense." Let's face it. That could happen. (smile) Typically at the end of a meeting like this, we decide whether or not we do
_____ (insert your ideal outcome here).

Prospect: Okay.

You: Okay, let's do this. Anything less than you thinking, "Let's do _____" (take the ideal step you just outlined) is a great idea, let's call it a "No." Is that okay?

Prospect: Sure.

BIGGEST FEAR

(Manage any other expectations that you need to cover.)

You: My biggest fear is _____. If that's the case, do you mind if we talk about that now?[4]

---

[4] Fill in the blank with something you tell them that is about them, not about you.

Warning: When you set an opening agreement for the first time, it's going to feel like it takes an hour just to set up the rules of engagement! In reality, this takes only about two to three minutes. It's going to feel like it takes forever because it's new to you, and it's a step you've never taken. However, by doing so, you are creating a level playing field with your prospect that will shorten your sales cycle and help you avoid the prospect's system.

One last thing: Chances are if someone becomes defensive, aggressive or otherwise refuses to agree on the terms of the meeting, that's a big red flag and a sign that they're not a good prospect for you right now. Don't be afraid to say (gently), "Hmmm, I'm struggling here. If we can't even agree about what we're supposed to be accomplishing today, is there any reason to keep meeting?" Take it as a gift that they're letting you know now that it's not going to be a fit so you can call it a "No" and move on to the next prospect.

CHAPTER THREE CHECKLIST

* Review TADB, and complete an opening agreement at your next sales call.

* Think hard about your ideal outcome. Write it down. Have the courage at the meeting to ask for your ideal outcome.

* When you get to the end of a sales call and your prospect says anything other than "I'm in. Let's do this!" call it a "No." Remember, the decision to not make a

decision ("Let me think it over," "Let me sleep on it," "I need to check with my partner" or "Call me in a week" are just slow "No's." Rip the Band Aid off, and call it a *"No."*

❖   ❖   ❖

CHAPTER FOUR

YOUR QUESTIONING ARSENAL

Getting to know your prospect is essential, but don't think looking them up on Google, LinkedIn or Facebook is enough. The best way to *really* know a prospect—how they think and feel, what their business needs or doesn't and what they're committed to change (if anything)—is face to face (which includes over video).

As important as the facts are, you must dig deeper than that. You must know what they think about their current situation and, even more important, how it makes them feel.

Understanding your prospect's opinions is critical. Two people in the exact same situation may choose to handle things completely differently, based upon their life experience and view about the future. Our job is to enter these sales conversations with a childlike curiosity—not to project our own values or beliefs on the prospect. It's never about us, the seller.

Remember the story of my buddy whose house caught fire? Firemen dumped thousands of gallons of water into his house to extinguish the flames. Four years later, he was still fighting with his insurance company about who was going to pay for what in the renovation. Even if a solution seems obvious—house catches fire, call 911—never assume it's the right solution for your prospect.

As sellers, we need to keep our own opinions to ourselves until we've fully explored our prospect's beliefs, biases and judgments.

In this chapter, I'll teach you how to get to know a prospect and their opinions using six No BS questioning strategies. Of course, there's no one way to do this. Instead, there are numerous strategies to employ using your No BS Sales mindset.

UNDERSTAND YOUR PROSPECT'S SITUATION

Remember that Will Smith movie *Hitch*? There's a scene that perfectly demonstrates the power of asking great questions, ones that bring out opinions and help you stay engaged but not emotionally involved.

The setting: upscale urban bar, low lighting, softly pulsing club track. Will Smith's character, the dating coach Alex "Hitch" Hitchens, eyes a beautiful woman sitting alone. He begins by asking the bartender questions. Among other things, Hitch learns the woman is a newspaper columnist who usually orders a beer. This evening, however, she's drinking a Grey Goose martini, dirty. Armed with this intel and plenty of acute observations that show he's paying attention, he walks over to meet her.

But another contender gets to her first. Hard-charging Chip has his lines memorized, and he isn't going to take no for an answer. "I noticed your glass was getting kind of low, so I took the liberty of bringing you another apple martini," he says, proving he wasn't paying close enough attention. "And I couldn't help but notice, you look a lot like my next girlfriend." (It was so awkward that it made me grind my teeth.)

Sara is totally not interested and lets Chip know, using clear language. She's even nice about it—except for one witty jab ("What's your name?" she asks. "They call me 'Chip,'" he says. "Aww, you can't get 'em to stop?") But Chip just doesn't listen. He keeps trying to woo her with lame bullshit and trap her with yes/no questions.

When Hitch steps up, the contrast between the two men is clear. Hitch is emotionally detached and nimble and has an air of charisma without seeming to try too hard. He engages in a way that recognizes *her*. He doesn't attempt to take over the conversation. Nor does he surrender all the control. He comes off as honest and genuinely interested without being needy—and then he walks away, and we see that she is interested.

This scene is a great example of two different sales styles as well. Based on those, how would you respond if you ran into a salesperson acting like Chip? A guy pressuring you and trying to get you to close as quickly as possible with a canned script? If you were engaged in conversation by someone like Hitch, confident and agile in his approach, would you be more open to a future meeting, even if now wasn't the right time?

In my first job out of college, I worked at a bank. I'd been told my whole life that I should go into sales, which I learned later was code for "You talk too much and try too hard to get people to like you." Not yet understanding the code, I was excited to put my skills to use in the bank.

I had this boss, Frank, who was a couple years older than me, and he took me on sales calls so I could begin to learn how to sell the bank's way. Frank, bless his heart, would always tell me, "Walker, you just gotta ask the right questions." I would go on sales calls with him, and I would pay attention, but I never picked up which were the "right" questions. I'd see him asking about the pictures on their desk, the fish on the wall or what they thought about the game last weekend, and so I did that, too.

He'd then jump into a pitch about why the prospect should move their relationship to us.

Then he'd watch me on a sales call. Afterwards, he'd say, "No, you didn't ask the right questions."

Finally, one day I said to him, "Frank, what in the hell are the right questions?"

He looked at me and shook his head, said, "You'd know if you had been paying attention."

I realized then that I needed to get the hell out of the banking business. Frank was never going to teach me anything. Yep, Frank—I'm still telling that story.

After I left my bank job, I went on a quest to learn, among other things, what the right questions are. And I realized there is no objective set of "right questions." What I needed to learn was my prospect's opinions about their current situation and what (if anything) they'd be committed to change. Over time, I developed a series of questioning strategies to help me connect with prospects and clients in a meaningful way.

There are a few different types of questioning strategies in the No BS Sales System that should get you started with the ask-don't-tell mindset established in the earlier chapters. As I mentioned previously, every sales coach/sales manager/sales guru will tell you, "Ask more questions." Since you're reading this book, I'm sure you're already asking questions—probably lots of them. But are you asking the questions that can give you the information you need to qualify or disqualify the prospect in front of you? In this chapter, I'm going to share some of the questions and questioning strategies you can put to use today to help you find the gap between where your prospect currently is and where they want to be.

Since no two sales situations are alike, here are six different questioning strategies to get the truth from your prospects and clients. Remember, the goal is to have them share their opinions about their situation. By doing so, you will help your prospects and clients explore ideas that no one else is helping them explore. This action of helping others process their current situation out loud will build not only understanding between you but also trust.

SIX QUESTIONING STRATEGIES

1. Good/Bad

This questioning strategy is key when you're attempting to unseat an incumbent relationship. You may know why you and your product or service is better than what they have, but unless those differentiators matter to the prospect, you don't have anything. With this and all of our questioning strategies, unless the prospect says it, unless it actually comes out of their mouth, it's not true to them. Once they do say it, however, it is their truth.

I believe that most people don't know what "good" looks like, and they just assume that what they've been getting is "normal."

Why do they think that? Think about how crappy salespeople sell.

They'll say things like, "We've got the best service. We've got the best product. We've got the best people."

Okay, sounds good. How many of your competitors say, "Our service sucks, our product is clearly inferior, and our people have worse DNA than the average citizen"?

Not many, I'd bet.

So, what's a prospect to believe?

It must all be about the same. Only difference must be price.

I mean, think about the person you buy insurance from for your home and cars right now. If I asked you, "How is your relationship with your insurance person?" you'd probably answer, "It's fine." The truth is you probably never think about her unless it's time to re-up your premium or you have a claim. Then, whatever happens, you probably just assume the service you experience with them is probably about what everyone experiences, frustrations and all. Maybe you shop around for price every now and then because if service is the same everywhere, price is all that matters.

If you happen to sell home and auto insurance, and you don't want to be the person who is always cheaper, this can be a problem. You have to find out what's going on now in your prospect's current situation to see if they have a reason to spend more, not less, to hire you.

Questions out of the blue like, "What do you not like about your current provider?" with no context are not going to get you much useful information. It will usually just make your prospect defensive. Slow down, and earn the right to explore things like this, but not in those words.

You need to give them space to explore what they like and don't like about their current relationship. They probably don't think about it that much.

Begin by complimenting your prospect on their current choice. "Oh, you're working with *ABC Company*. I hear they're great (even if you've never heard of them or if you know they've got problems)." Then try to draw out specifics: "I'm curious: What do you like about what *ABC Company* does for you?"

Why would I want my prospect to say out loud what they like about my competition? A couple of reasons: 1) If they like something my competitor is doing, they're probably going to look for that from me if they switch. I want to know their expectations early, and 2) it's great competitor intel. Don't you want to know what they're up to?

Once they tell you one thing they like, keep asking—"Great, what else?"—until they get to the point where they say something to the effect of, "Well, that's about all I can think of."

Bonus points if you can repeat their points back to them:

"So, you say you like the personal touch, they let you know in advance before they do anything and you love the color of their trucks. That's great."

Now you need to say, "You know, I've heard that about them," or, "They're known for that." Nothing builds bonding with your prospect like validation of their opinions, telling them they're smart for the decision they've already made! This may feel as abhorrent to you as licking a dirty floor, but who are we to tell them their opinions are wrong?

Once you've learned what they like about the current relationship, you've earned the right to ask the follow-up:

"Here's what I know. We're not perfect. I can't imagine those folks are perfect. If there were one thing you wish they did better or differently, what would that be?" Your exact wording matters here. Notice I'm asking for "one thing" and not using wishy-washy language like "anything" or "something."[5]

We're asking a specific question (one thing) to get a specific answer. Asking a general question using words like "something" or "anything" will most likely only get you a general and vague answer like "I don't know" or "I can't think of anything."

When my boys were little, I used to take them out for pancakes on Saturday mornings. When I would go to pay the bill, the lady behind the register would ask how the breakfast was, and I would simply say it was fine. If she asked, "Mr. McKay, if there was one thing we could do to make your breakfast better, what would that be?" I'd say, "Your coffee sucks." If you want to know specifics, ask for specifics. People are happy to share if you make them comfortable that you're not judging and you ask specific questions.

Here's another subtlety: When they share things they don't like, be surprised, and keep asking, "What else?" If you jump on the first thing, you might not get to the real problem.

This whole process is meant to build rapport so that you understand what's going on with your prospect.

---

[5] Equally important is how you say it—your tone. When you ask this question, or any question for that matter, ask it in a way that makes you sound sincerely curious. You'll nail it if you say it in a way that makes you sound like you just thought of the question.

TALKING POINTS: GOOD/BAD ROLE PLAY

All change is hard. No matter how great you think your stuff is and how much better this prospect will be once they become your client, your prospect has to get over their fear, uncertainty and doubt about change. Your competitors have poisoned the well by continually promising "better service, better quality, better value"—and then delivering none of that. If you look, sound or feel like other salespeople to your prospect, you're going to get treated like them. (Revisit the "Introduction: The Prospect's Trap," if you're not sure what being treated like a standard salesperson is like.) Being different requires an open mind, humility and sincere curiosity. In the following scenario, notice how gently I ask the questions and how I nimbly roll with Jenny when she gives answers.

Walker: So, Jenny, you said you had a sales coach before. Who was that?

Jenny: Danielle Avatar.

Walker: Oh, wow. She's famous. How long did you work with her?

Jenny: For about a year.

Walker: I've heard she's really, really good. What did *you* like best about her?

Jenny: I loved her approach. She wasn't pushy. She was good at letting me come up with answers on my own. She has a book with some great strategies.

Walker: She's known as somebody who's kind and who cares about her folks. And, yeah, her book is a great guide. You're lucky to have worked with her.

Jenny: Yes, it was a great experience.

Walker: Here's my guess, though. I'm not perfect in what I do, and I can't imagine that she was perfect. If there were one thing you wish she'd done better or differently, what would that be?

Jenny: Well, even though she was a great human—and I felt like she taught me a lot about sales—I never got tangible results from the coaching.

Walker: Huh. That's weird. Surely you got results.

Jenny: My sales didn't increase much at all. I paid all this money, and nothing really changed. That was disappointing.

Walker: Okay. Well, I get that. What else?

Jenny: Well, I got the feeling, especially toward the end of our contract period, that she was spending more time selling me to rejoin than she was actually trying to help me grow.

Walker: Huh. That surprises me, too. Anything else?

Jenny: No, that's about it.

Walker: Okay, tell me more about "*selling* you instead of *coaching* you." Can you give me an example?

Notice that I didn't bite on the first thing she told me. Had I done that, I might not have learned about the "selling instead of coaching" problem. Now that I have a couple of problems "out on the table," I can take each one and run it through the "Pain Test" to see if either of those things are compelling enough for her to make a change. More on the Pain Test in "Chapter Five: Discover and Disqualify."

2. Reversing with softening statements

When I first started doing sales training, the VP of sales of a large company asked me if I did in-person training.

Damn, I thought as my heart sank in anticipation of her response to my answer. I did *all* my training over Zoom. This was years ago, before most people knew what Zoom was. I was worried that once I started explaining how online training worked, she'd be skeptical.

I paused, about to say something like, "Well, I guess I could."

Instead, I said, "I appreciate you asking that question. You must be asking for a reason."

"I am," she said. "We have offices in five different cities, and it's too expensive for us to bring people together. We'd prefer if you could do some sort of video-conference training."

"As a matter of fact," I said, "we use this great new technology platform called Zoom."

Thank goodness I took the time to learn what the real question was. That helped me land them as a client that I've kept for many years.

Before you answer a question, make sure you know what your prospect is *really* trying to learn. To find out, use reversing statements.

Think of "reversing" as basically answering a question with a question. The point of this questioning strategy is to clarify what the other person *really* wants to know.

To me, being in a sales call is a bit like clinging to the top of a frozen mountain peak with plunging ice walls on all sides. As long as I'm asking questions, I have an ice axe anchored deep to keep me from being blown off. When I start *answering* questions, that anchor loosens, and I'm much more vulnerable to getting blown off.

That icy peak is a metaphor for trust between you and your prospect. In that sales call, your prospect is deciding whether or not you're someone they can trust. One of the fastest ways to break trust is to give an answer early on that disqualifies you in their mind.

For example, I get asked a fair amount, "Have you worked with any of my competitors?" I've been doing sales training for more than 20 years and have worked with at least 1,000 companies in more than 100 industries. Chances are, I have, but I want to know why they're asking. So I'll ask them back, "That's an interesting question. You must be asking that for a reason."

Prospect: "Yeah, because I want to know if you understand my industry."

To which I might reply, "That makes sense. What part of your industry were you hoping I understood?"

Prospect: "Well, our business is different [everyone thinks their business is different], and I'd want you to know X and Y."

At that point, I could keep reversing until he had explained the specific problems he and his sales team are encountering right now in their industry.

Imagine being slammed with work, and your prospect says, "When could we start?" In order to give "great customer service," you may answer, "Right away," even if you know it's going to cause chaos in your shop to pull that off. How would you feel later if you found out you lost the deal because your prospect needed a month to get ready and you never asked? (Insert your own cuss words here _____.)

A better response is, "I appreciate your asking that. When were you hoping we could get started?"

This way, at least you know the real question.

One of my clients, an experienced seller of expensive and complicated communications equipment, loves the reversing strategy when she gets asked about price too early in the conversation, like before she knows what the real issues are. She responds with, "Thanks for asking that. Price sounds like it must be important to you if you're asking about it. Tell me why you're asking *now*."

She says sometimes her prospects tell her their budget, and others reveal themselves as really needing only a price check to keep their current vendor "honest."

THE POWER OF SOFTENING STATEMENTS

You've probably noticed I'm not exactly answering a question with "just another question." I'm also using softening statements. Softening statements are words or phrases you apply before using your reversing question. By using them, you avoid sounding like you're interrogating your prospect, and it also gives you time to think. (Thinking. Crazy idea, right?)

Examples of softening statements:

- Good question
- Good point
- Thanks for asking that

- Makes sense
- I hear that a lot
- Smart
- That's a good one
- Ah, yes
- Good observation
- And that means
- Sounds like that's important
- You must be asking that for a reason
- I understand
- Interesting question
- I like the way you think
- I'm really glad you asked that

I do an exercise with my clients in which I get two of them to face each other and ask each other questions. One asks a question, and then the other asks a non-related question back. No answering the question and no repeating of a question. It sounds like, "How's the weather?" and the response is, "Do you play golf?" and then "Where were you born?" and on from there.

This is a rapid-fire exercise, and most people don't make it past three or four questions. Next, I ask them to do the same thing again, but this time use softening statements, and ask back an unrelated question. "What color is the sky?" and then "Great question. Glad you asked. What is your favorite food?"

and on and on. Often, we can get to seven or eight questions per person before it gets too tedious.

The last exercise is the same as before, but each person can give a softening statement, answer the question and then ask a non-related question back. This last exercise is much easier, as each person has more time to think. I'll let this go on for a little while—it gets annoying as shit for everyone—just so they can see how much easier it is with a little bit of space to think between questions.

Here's the thing about reversing. Sometimes people just want you to answer the question. They may find the reversing aggravating. Here's my rule. If someone asks you the same question three times, just answer it.

Prospect: "How much does it cost?"

You: "Glad you asked. You must be asking that now for a reason."

Prospect: "Yeah, I want to know how much it costs."

You: "It's expensive (one of my favorite responses!). Tell me why you're asking."

Prospect: "Just tell me how much it costs."

You: "Happy to do so. It's _____."

I like to say, "It's expensive" when asked how much my services cost. It's definitely a pattern interrupt. I never want to sound arrogant, but I tell them that to prepare them.[6]

When you do give them the number, they say either, "That's not so bad," and you can be wrong and win anyway, or they say, "Holy shit! That's crazy!" and you can say (laughing), "I told you so."

If you are plagued by price shoppers, you can add something to your upfront agreement. "My biggest fear," you can say, "is

---

[6] It's expensive only if it doesn't work!

that you're hoping we're going to be the cheapest option. If that's what you're thinking, let's talk about that right now so I don't waste your time." You're essentially getting vulnerable with your prospect to allow them to also become more comfortable sharing their opinions and overall situation with you.

TALKING POINTS: REVERSING USING SOFTENING STATEMENTS

Reversing questions help you truly understand what your prospect is trying to learn from you. Softening statements soften what might otherwise sound like an interrogation. The other bonus is that they also give you time to think. It's okay to string a couple of the softening statements together.

Prospect: When would your program start?

You: Good question. You must be asking that for a reason.

Prospect: Yeah, my people are going to be traveling for the next couple of weeks, and I'd like to delay the start until then.

Prospect: How would you handle "X"?

You: That's a good one. How were you *hoping* we would handle that?

Prospect: Well, I'd like for you to do it this way.

You: Okay—glad you shared that. Tell me why doing it that way is important to you.

Prospect: What kind of warranty does this have?

You: That's a great question. Why do you ask?

Prospect: I was just wondering. I think most of those warranties are worthless.

You: I hear that a lot. Sounds like you've got a good story. Do you mind sharing it?

Prospect: Who would be assigned to our account?

You: I'm really glad you asked that. Tell me why you asked that right now.

Prospect: We've heard really good things about Sam. It would be great to have him on our team.

3. Third-party stories

Stories are a part of being human. This is why we enjoy books and movies, and why many legends, myths and historical accounts are still being told today. I've already warned you about sharing your opinions too early in a sales call. And I know what you're thinking: *Walker, how do I tell people what we do or what they should do without sharing my opinion? At some point, I have to tell them something, right?*

Yes. In a sales call, you can talk 30% of the time, and they should talk 70%. If you want to make a point, don't say it like, "Well, our cool thing is better than their cool thing." Why? Because whatever opinion you share is going to be discounted as sales bullshit. No one cares what you think. They do care, however, what other people like them think.

Think about the difference between, "We've got the best customer service" and "A lot of our clients tell us that our customer service is the best they've ever experienced." The first one sounds like you're bragging, while the other is being presented in the form of something like a review.

What if you're new in sales and lacking in personal third-party stories of your own? One option is to borrow from others in your firm. Ask around for examples of great things clients say about the company in general. Use those until you build your own stockpile by taking note of positive feedback from clients.

There are three usual situations where third-party stories can be helpful. First, if you want to promote your positives: Third-party stories let you say nice things about yourself or the company without coming across as arrogant or bragging. This is why you'll see testimonials and other reviews on a company's website, for example. It's a quick and easy way to give your prospects a glimpse of what you can do best.

The second situation is when you want to find out a prospect's problem, but you don't want to sound like you're judging them for it. "I talk to people in your business all the time, and they tell me they're struggling because their competition is lowballing prices, and it's hard to keep their margins and still win business. My guess is that you're not facing those issues." You're giving them the comfort of telling their situation by letting them know, 1) that you're familiar with their business and, 2) that other people are having this problem, too. This allows you to say, "I didn't think so," if they're not having that problem or to act surprised if they say, "Yeah, we are having that problem."

The third situation is when you want to show your experience or even set a precedent. This typically works because no one wants to be the guinea pig. Let's say it's time to talk about the budget. You quote a price, and your prospect's face goes white; they say, "Dayumm, that's expensive!"

Imagine the prospect's response if you said, "Yeah, but it's worth every penny." Talk about sales bullshit!

Instead, you can respond with, "You're right. And I hear that sometimes. I have a client in your business who hired me about a year ago. He was sweating bullets when he signed the agreement and made his first payment. Ten months later, he said it turned out to be the best money he'd ever spent. He said he'd gotten a 5x return on his investment in training."

Here, you're letting them know that they're not alone in their feelings and that you've helped others who felt the same way.

Here's one of my favorite ways to use a third-party story: When you feel stuck in a sales call, describe the prospect in a third-party way. "I was talking to a guy just like you about a month ago. He was worried about the same thing. He finally said, 'If I don't spend the money now, it's only going to cost me more in the future.' You may not feel that way, though."

Remember, no one cares about your opinion until they've paid you for it. If you want to tell somebody something, tell them what someone else said.

You may have noticed I used a "takeaway" at the end of those stories. I gave the prospect the "out" that they may not be experiencing what the other person like them was experiencing. The purpose of all of our questions is not to lead the prospect, but to get to the truth.

Any time you want to share your opinion, say something nice about yourself or your company, or make a point to help move your sale forward, use a third-party story. Other people's opinions count way more than your own.

4. Assumptive questions

As the name suggests, with an assumptive question, you make an assumption that something has happened or will likely happen and frame your question around it.

Sound confusing? Here's an example: "When your financial advisor sits with you, goes over your statements and asks about your life to make the necessary adjustments to your portfolio, how does that go?" The question assumes all these things have taken place.

Maybe your prospect will say, "Well, my advisor doesn't actually do that." Remember, most people don't know what *good* looks like. They know only what they've been getting. By using assumptive questions, you can begin to differentiate yourself and your company without sounding like you're bragging.

Other examples:

When they told you their warranty doesn't cover any of the moving parts, the ones that break the most often, how did they make you comfortable with that?

When their rep told you that all of their customer-service functions were now online-chat only and that there wasn't even a phone number for you to call, how did you make sense of that?

But what if your competitor is doing things well? The financial advisor is sitting down with the prospect, going over statements quarterly and asking about life changes that might inform portfolio adjustments? Assumptive questions can help you learn that before you start making similar claims that will fall flat. If they say, "Yeah, my financial advisor does that, and here's what happened last time," you can say, "Great, that was a smart move." You're not pinned down, as you would have been if you said from the start, "We meet with our clients four times a year to go over your stuff and see if we need to make any changes," without having any idea if they're getting that or even want that kind of service.

I already mentioned that I do much of my sales training online. That was an early differentiator for me. Long before the Zoom boom, I noticed that companies often had salespeople in four, five, even ten different cities. It didn't take much to realize what a pain in the neck and how expensive it was to bring people together in one place.

So, I asked a prospect, "When [the incumbent company] conducted their sales training and made it virtual so you'd need only an internet connection to start, how did it work out?"

"Huh? That never happened," they said. "Everyone had to travel and meet in one place."

I gave them the idea that doing the training virtually would have been much more convenient and, more important, less expensive. It was a more sophisticated way to make the point.

And more surgically precise. What if I were an insurance salesman and asked, "How's your relationship with your insurance agent?" You'd probably shrug your shoulders and say, "Fine."

But what if I asked: "When your insurance agent sat down with you last year to go over the contents of your home—the items of value you may have sold or acquired—to make sure you're properly covered and not over-insured and paying too much, what kind of changes did they make?"

That question forces specificity and lets you identify your competitor's shortcomings without pointing them out directly.

Another situation in which you can use assumptive questions is to find out if your prospect has already considered future steps. Remember, as a guide, you need to help them figure out what best to do next. Therefore, you could ask: "When you talk to your business partner about what we've discussed, what do you think he will say?" You're opening a door to brainstorm a future conversation.

How about when a prospect is asking for a concession of some kind? "I'll be happy to check with the boss about that. When I do, he's going to ask if there's anything else you might need to make a decision. What should I tell him when he asks that?"

"When you asked your mom that, what did she say?" is one of my favorite questions for my children. It cuts through their bullshit quickly.

TALKING POINTS: SHOW 'EM WHAT GOOD LOOKS LIKE

Me: Dave, you're married, right?

Dave: Yup

Me: Happily married?

Dave: Yes, of course.

Me: Great—I thought so. So, on Friday nights, when you come home and your wife greets you and says, "Honey,

I'm so glad you're here. I sent the kids to my mother's house, just poured you a drink and turned on ESPN in the man cave. Why don't you go watch SportsCenter while I get dinner ready. I'm cooking your favorite meal." When that happens every Friday night, what's that favorite meal of yours that she makes?

Dave: Um, who are we talking about? That never happens.

5. Let's pretend

Ever want to know what your prospect might think about something that hasn't happened yet? Use the "Let's pretend" strategy.

This can be as simple as saying, "Let's pretend it's a year from now and you say to me, 'Walker, working with you was the greatest decision I've made.' What would have to happen in the next 12 months for you to be able to say that to me?" It's a powerful question that makes your prospect think about what they actually want to accomplish and the outcomes they expect from working with you. It's like those trial balloons politicians use to float ideas and see what kind of response they get.

You can also use this strategy to keep from dying the death of a thousand cuts. Have you ever experienced a prospect who seems like they never want the sales call to end because they keep asking for more?

Prospect: You need to sharpen your pencil. Your price is too high!

You: Okay. I can give you a 10% discount.

Prospect: Great. I want to finance it over a longer term.

You: Okay. How long?

Prospect: Thirty-six months, not twenty-four.

You: Boss said we can do that. Okay.

Prospect: I want free delivery.

You: Okay.

I mean, this can be absolutely brutal for the seller, but it's a very effective strategy if you're a buyer.

What if you responded to the first question this way instead: "Let's pretend we can agree on price. What else would you need to see or hear from me to be able to make a decision?"

This way, you can learn what other hurdles you might have to overcome.

Or how about during a negotiation, when your prospect asks you to give up something? To see how strongly they feel about it without committing to doing it, you could ask, "Let's pretend we couldn't get that approved. Is it over?" If they say, "Yeah, it's over," you can always respond with, "Okay—let's pretend we could get that approved. What happens next?"

Let's pretend scenarios allow them to think beyond their current situation and tell you what they'd do or expect in the future if certain things happen or don't happen.

6. Columbo questions

Columbo, played by the Academy Award-nominated actor Peter Falk, was a 1970s television icon. The character was a grumpy, disheveled detective who looked like he slept in his clothes. He came off as if he didn't know what he was doing, but he was always able to catch the culprit by asking unexpected and sometimes dumb-sounding questions. In short, he was dumb like a fox.

Columbo questions may feel like dumb questions, but they're a very effective tool to get your prospect to clarify their previous statements or to get an opinion.

Here are a few examples:

Prospect: Our margins are at 30%.
You: Where would you hope they would be?

Prospect: We've had lots of turnover.
You: When you say, "lots of turnover," what do you mean?

Prospect: We're going to get three quotes.
You: Thanks for telling me. Why are you getting three quotes?

You can see how this can be hard, right? You have to do it gently, or else the prospect might misunderstand and get mad. Asking a Columbo question will challenge your prospect, but not in a rude way, to see what would happen next.

Ten years ago, I had a sales call with a prospect who owned a small insurance firm. He said he had three salesmen working for him and that things were smooth and steady. I Columbo'd up a bit and said, "It sounds like everything is going great. What were you hoping I could help you with?"

"My exit strategy."

Once again, I Columbo'd up: "Your exit strategy?"

"Yeah," he said. "I'm hoping to retire in five or six years, but I'm worried about the value of the business when it's time to sell."

"The value of the business?" I asked, repeating the last five words of his statement phrased as a question. I needed him to say why he was worried.

And that opened the floodgates. He vomited information for 30 minutes. It turns out he was the top producer in his firm by far. When he was ready to retire, he knew that any buyer would heavily discount his book since he wouldn't be around to service it anymore, which increased the risk that his top-revenue clients might leave. In order to get the money he knew he needed to retire, he'd need not only the other producers to sell more, but he'd also need to hire more producers. He said he'd need to transition to being more of a manager/leader instead of a player/coach.

Those were his conclusions. Those were his thoughts. I didn't have to share any of mine. I occasionally would chime in "What else?" or "And then what?" to keep him going.

Once he'd shared his situation with me and his opinions about it, I had no problem finding his pain. (More about that in the next chapter.)

Being dumb like Columbo got me a client that put me on retainer for three years. He sold his business for about 40% more than he told me he'd hoped to get when we first met. He also referred me to four more business owners, two of whom have hired me since then.

Another time Columbo questions come in handy is when someone shares problems but doesn't seem concerned about fixing them. If you feel it, say it: "I'm confused. You've shared all of these problems, but none seems important enough to fix. What am I missing?"

The question puts the focus on them to explain the part that you don't understand and again share their opinions.

Be gentle when using Columbo questions.

THE BOY WHO KNEW TOO MUCH

Jimmy was 16 when he landed a summer job at the local hardware store. He was excited but nervous because he didn't know anything about anything in that store. On day one, his manager said, "Look, kid, I don't have time to train you. You're signed up to go to hardware-product school in two weeks. Until then, just sit in this chair and, if somebody asks you for help, do what you can, and try not to screw it up."

He didn't have to wait long. An elderly lady—leaning on a cane, eyes darting back and forth behind Coke-bottle glasses—walked in and said, "Son, can you help me please? I need a heater for my house, and I don't know what kind to buy or where to find it."

Jimmy jumped up and said he'd love to help. Then he panicked, because he didn't know anything about heaters or even where they were in the store! As he walked down the rows looking for heaters, he just started asking her questions. Why was she looking for a heater? Where was she going to use it in her house?

She told him the room in the back of her house, where she watched television, was always cold, and she wanted something to take the chill off.

He found the heater aisle but panicked again when he saw the many choices—big heaters, small heaters, ceramic heaters, electric heaters, all in different colors and prices.

He began to explain the many options, but she stopped him and said, "Which one do you recommend?"

"I don't know," he said, being honest. "Can I ask you a few more questions?"

"Of course," she said.

"How much money do you want to spend? We've got heaters from $25 to $200 here."

"Well," she said, "I don't want the cheapest one because it might catch my house on fire, but $200 is probably more than I need to spend. How about around $100?"

"Perfect," he said and began to look at the $100 heaters. They came in multiple colors. Did she have a preference? She said her rug was blue and she didn't want to trip on it, so if there was a white one, she'd prefer that one.

Jimmy grabbed a white $100 heater and walked her to the register, where someone rang up the sale. As she was leaving, she thanked the young man and then walked to the manager's office. Once again, Jimmy panicked, thinking the elderly lady, his first customer, might tell the manager that he didn't know anything and should be fired.

Instead, she told the manager how much she appreciated the young man taking time to understand what she needed and then to offer her such good advice.

The boy and the manager beamed with pride.

Similar encounters happened over and over again during the next two weeks. Jimmy didn't know much, so he kept asking questions. His sales kept stacking up.

The manager looked at him the day he was leaving for product school and said, "Son, when you get back knowing all there is to know about everything in this store, the sky will be the limit for you. You'll sell as much as Carl, who's been here for years."

During his training, Jimmy soaked up knowledge about everything the store stocked, from asphalt shingles to zip ties and everything in between. He got a 100 on his exam and a certificate for his achievement. That piece of paper showed he was now officially "smart."

On his first day back at the store, Jimmy was amped, eager to help his first customer. A man walked in and said, "I need to buy a cooler."

"Follow me, sir," Jimmy said, marching the man to the cooler aisle. "We sell the best cooler in the world here, and today it's on sale. This thing is bear-proof, holds enough food for a family of four and keeps ice frozen for a week. It's usually $400, but it's on sale today for $320. What color would you like?"

The man, looking uncomfortable, thanked Jimmy for his time and said he'd need to think about it, but he'd be back. He never came back.

What Jimmy didn't know was that the man was taking his five-year-old grandson fishing. He was looking for a small, cheap cooler to keep a couple of sandwiches and drinks cool while they were in the boat. Jimmy had shared great product knowledge, but he'd made no attempt to learn what the customer needed and why.

This scenario repeated itself over and over, and Jimmy's sales plummeted. Why? Because Jimmy had made the jump from dummy to smart, and it had only hurt him.

Carl, meanwhile, made sale after sale by not telling everything he knew, but rather by asking dumb questions, like Columbo, to understand what the customer wanted and why they wanted it. He could then recommend a product that suited his customer perfectly. Carl was no dummy. He was a professional.

Use all six of these questioning strategies in your sales calls and in all aspects of your life to uncover opinions, beliefs and other truths that will help you become a better problem-solver and guide.

BE SKEPTICAL TO GET THE TRUTH:
USING NINJA QUESTIONS AND PHRASES

By this point, I bet you're pissed at me. You can't believe you wasted your money and time on this book. And you've certainly figured out that my No BS Sales System wouldn't work in your business.

Ha! *Gotcha.*

If you've read this far, I hope you're really thinking, *This shit is so good, I can't wait to go try it!*

But you're probably not there yet.

The point I'm setting up here is that using reverse psychology—doing the opposite of what your prospect expects—is a powerful way to get to the truth. One way to do that is using ninja questions and phrases, like the ones I used above.

Ninjas, as you may already know, were 15th-century Japanese mercenaries. Their appeal is so great, they remain a force in popular culture across movies, video games, TV shows, animations and more. One comic-book artist even adapted them into teenage mutant turtles who love pizza.

Ninjas were famous for many things, but one of them was how they fought. They operated stealthily and used their opponent's weight and speed against them. A foe rushes in, and the ninja makes a calculated sidestep, grips an arm and uses the opponent's momentum to spin them to the ground. With the No BS Sales System, ninja questions work in a similar way. You tell the prospect something so bizarre they will have to correct you. The whole point of ninja questions is for you to be wrong and them to be right, but you still win because you learned the truth.

It's common for salespeople to say things like "This is perfect for you" or "You're going to love it." How do you feel when someone says that to you? Probably skeptical, which is the normal response. Until someone has spent enough time understanding what you need, how can they know it will be perfect for you?

Instead, draw your prospects' opinions out by letting them correct you. Be honest with them. Say, "You know, I'm not entirely sure if you're going to like this or not, but. . . ." Not only will that approach help you get them to express what they want in more detail, but it will also allow you to build rapport much faster. You're not telling them what you think they need. You're giving them room to express themselves.

I used to do this all the time when I was still in commercial real estate. Before walking into any building or site I would say to my prospect, "This is not perfect, and you might not like it. As soon as you figure out that you don't like it, just let me know, and we can get out of here."

I was both managing expectations and opening a door for them to just tell me the truth. No pressure from me. If they said, "You were right—this place isn't the right fit," then I come across as more credible. If they say, "Actually, this place is really great!" I can get them to tell me what they like about it. Notice how different that is from declaring to the prospect what I thought was perfect for them or pressuring them to "like" something because I told them they should.

Make it easy for your prospect to disagree with you. It's human nature. Let them be right, and you still win.

Using ninja questions and phrases means using negative words like:

- Not
- Can't
- Won't
- Shouldn't
- Haven't
- No way
- Never
- Impossible

Or phrases like:

◈ There's probably no way . . .

◈ You are going to think this is a stupid idea . . .

◈ This probably is not the case with you . . .

◈ Sounds like it's over . . .

◈ Not a chance . . .

◈ This is going to sound ridiculous . . .

The power of these questions and phrases is that they're not expected. You won't sound like any other salesperson. You'll hear me use the phrase "pattern interrupt" a lot, because being negative, like being a ninja, takes the prospect's power and uses it against them. The goal of ninja questions and phrases, as with all of our questioning strategies, is to get the prospect to open up and talk. When they're talking, they feel like they're in control. But the person listening—you—is really in control. It's hard to disqualify a prospect who's not ready for you yet if you're the one doing all the talking and telling them all the reasons they should like what you're selling.

Imagine the question: "Why should I buy from you?"

An amateur salesperson might jump at the chance to say, "Well, we've got better people, better service and better quality"—just like all the other amateur salespeople say. Your prospect will tune out and not hear a word you said.

Better to say: "Well, maybe you shouldn't." One of the shortcomings of this book (and of all printed material) is that it's hard to share tone of voice. When you respond with a negative, you must sound kind and curious, not sarcastic. If you're naturally sarcastic, you might know the words to say, but your tone will be all wrong.

Why the negative? At this point, who are we to say that they should buy from us? We might not be the right fit for them or them for us.

Remember the old Scooby Doo cartoons, when good-natured Scooby would get surprised? His eyes would get big, and he would say, "Huh?" If you're executing your ninja questions right, you will get a lot of Scooby responses. You're not doing this to punk anybody, only to disarm them—break down their natural defense mechanisms—so both of you can be more genuine with one another. Then you can leverage that openness to get to know them better and explain more of your side as well.

If someone asks me what my services cost, I'll often respond, "A lot." No need to justify, defend or explain how much I charge.

Usually, if I've done a good job finding pain (next chapter!), and my prospect has the context of how much the problem is costing them, they'll say, "That's not as bad as I thought," to which I can respond, "Damn, I'd better raise my prices!"

Not many sellers will say "It's expensive" when asked "How much?" That's why I want you to say it.

Second, I'm managing expectations. *Expensive* means different things to different people. *It's always too expensive if someone doesn't need what you have.* I might as well lead them to believe it's expensive and let them tell me I was wrong. It's only a great value if the prospect says it is. My grandmother had this great expression: "It's not too expensive, Walker. You just can't afford it!"

And after telling them I charge a lot, when I do tell them my fee, it can go one of two ways. They might say, "Hell, that's not too much." In that case, once again I was wrong, they were right, and I win anyway. Or they say, "Oh, my God—that *is* a lot," and I say, "See, I told you so." Either way, I'm safe.

In one of my favorite episodes of the classic 1990s TV show *Seinfeld*, George discovers the almost-mystical power of doing the opposite of what he would normally do. One day, as George kvetches to Jerry and Elaine in Monk's Café, the neighborhood coffee shop, a beautiful blond perched at the counter glances at George. Elaine encourages him to talk to her.

"Elaine," George says. "Bald men with no jobs and no money who live with their parents don't approach strange women."

"Well, here's your chance to try the opposite," Jerry says. "Instead of tuna salad and being intimidated by women, chicken salad and going right up to them." If every instinct you have is wrong, Jerry reasons, then the opposite would have to be right.

So, instead of sitting and doing nothing and regretting it for the rest of the day, George decides to do something. And it works! Soon, he's dating Victoria.

The ninja strategy is all about winning by doing the opposite. But it's an advanced questioning strategy. At this point, you might not be ready for it.

Did you see what I did there? *Of course*, you're ready.

Well, even so, you're probably not interested in learning another way to use ninja questions and phrases, right?

Okay—you win. Here's another way.

Think about your prospects as falling into one of three buckets when you first make contact with them.

In the first bucket are the **positive prospects**. These are the people who've never bought from you before, but they tell you early on, "I am ready to buy. I've heard so many great things, and it's time for me to get on-board." Ever have one of those? I bet you have.

Positive prospects are your most dangerous prospects. Yup. You read that right. Dangerous. They will waste a ton of your time. And it's all your fault. See, when you talk to a positive prospect who's "ready to go," you skip steps. You'll say to yourself, "This one is different. I don't have to do that No BS crap. This one is a layup."

And what inevitably happens? There's a problem. No budget, unrealistic expectations, a contract they can't get out of, horrible to work with. Or, you might just make an expensive mistake like I did.

I have a dear friend, Bryan, who refers a lot of business to me. He helps larger companies put on sales events. He gets the venue and does all the logistics. He's often asked to bring in speakers. A good connection for me, right? Plus, he's a great guy.

A couple of months ago, he called me and said he had a gig for me. Five hundred salespeople who worked for a large investment firm were meeting in Nashville for a conference. The CEO asked Bryan to recommend a speaker on sales. Bryan said, "I've got the guy for you." When Bryan called, he said this was a slam dunk. He'd already sent the guy a link to my website and a couple of episodes of the No BS Sales School podcast, which, he said, the CEO loved. He'd suggested a fee that was at the top of the range I'd been paid before, so that was great. He told me that the CEO had already approved my slot on the itinerary.

He just wanted to have a brief chat with me first. It was just a check-the-box thing, Bryan assured me. "No way I could screw this one up," I said, chuckling.

Right out of the gate, the CEO said, "I have heard so many great things about you from Bryan, and I have to tell you, I've really enjoyed listening to your podcast!" I'm sure I beamed with pride. He asked me what topic I thought would be a good one for his team at the conference, and I launched. "Well, the people in your business need blah, blah, blah, and I think this would be a good blah blah blah." Twenty minutes later, at the end of the call, the CEO said, "Wow, it's been great talking to you. Here's the thing, though: We have another speaker who is going to cover a similar topic, so I think we're going to stick with him."

We hung up, and I almost threw up. What in the hell was I doing? I know better!!! I fell for the positive-prospect trap. Me! The guy who wrote this book. What a moron I am. I know better.

Here's how the call should have gone:

Prospect: I have heard so many great things about you from Bryan, and I have to tell you, I've really enjoyed listening to your podcast!

Me: Wow. Thanks for telling me that. What did Bryan tell you?

Prospect: He said y'all work together a lot and that you'd be a great speaker for our conference.

Me: Okay—and you *believed* him? (laugh)

Prospect: Yeah, I've known Bryan for years.

Me: Well, here's what I know. Just because Bryan recommends me doesn't necessarily mean that I'm going to be the right fit to speak at your conference. Do you mind if I ask you a couple of questions to make sure I'm not wasting your time?

Prospect: Sure.

Me: Well, let's pretend you hired me, and I've just finished my talk at your conference. You're walking up to me, saying, "Wow. That was exactly the message I'd hope you'd give my team." What would I need to convey to your folks during my time onstage that would make you want to tell me that?

See how that might have made things turn out a little differently? If I'd been a little skeptical, used a pattern interrupt and then asked a couple of questions, I might have been able to turn that layup into a paying gig instead of an expensive lesson. That one still stings.

In the next bucket are the **neutral prospects**. They're the ones who, when you call them, will say things like, "How about sending me some information?" or "We're not really looking to change, but call us back next quarter." That last comment is code for, "You can have unlimited access to my voicemail if you'd like." You know this type well if you're doing any prospecting. Once again, your best strategy for prospects like this is to be skeptical, to do the opposite of what they expect, to be ninja.

Prospect: Well, why don't you send me some information and we'll look it over? (Translation: "I'd like to get you off of the phone.")

Untrained salesperson 🐼: Great. What's your email address? When can I call you back?

No BS Salesperson: I'd be happy to send you some information—(always say you're happy to, even if you're not going to; it's a good softening statement)—but I'm not sure what to send you. Do you mind if I ask you a question?

Prospect: Sure.

No BS Salesperson: We have thousands of documents I could send, but I'd hate to clog up your inbox with all of it. If there was one thing in particular you'd like to see from us, what would it be?

Prospect: Pricing info.

No BS Salesperson: Well, I can send you pricing, but you're probably not going to like it. We're going to be more expensive than what you have now.

Prospect: Well, I'm not interested.

No BS Salesperson: Makes sense. I'll let you go and close your file. Before I do, though, may I ask you one last question?

Prospect: Sure.

No BS Salesperson: If you had to come up with one reason to spend one dollar more than what you're currently paying, what would that be?

Prospect: Better service.

No BS Salesperson: I didn't see you picking that. Tell me more.

You may have noticed the pattern I was using: softening statement + negative statement + "Let me ask you a question" + question.

Here's the pattern applied to the first bucket.

Positive prospect: I'm ready to buy! You guys have helped a bunch of my friends.

Untrained salesperson 🐼: Let me tell you all about it!

No BS Salesperson: (softening statement) Great! Thanks for letting me know. (negative statement) I gotta tell you, though, just because you've heard we've helped other people doesn't necessarily mean we'd be the right fit for you. ("Let me ask you a question.") Do you mind if I ask you a couple of questions to make sure I'm not wasting your time?

Positive Prospect: Sure. Please do.

No BS Salesperson: (question) What did you hear from other people that made you think you should talk to us?

Now let's hit the third bucket, the **negative prospects.** Certainly there are varying degrees of negative, but let's start with an easy one.

Negative prospect: We're already working with someone who does what you do.

Untrained Salesperson 🐼: Okay. Can I call you next year? (Never ask permission to call a prospect back. Just freaking call them.)

No BS Salesperson: (softening statement) Thanks for letting me know. I appreciate that. (negative statement) If you're already working with someone you trust, you probably shouldn't switch. ("Let me ask you a question.") Do you mind if I ask you a question before I let you go?

Negative prospect: Sure.

No BS Salesperson: (question) Who are you working with?

Negative prospect: Jones and Company.

No BS Salesperson: Jones and Company. Those guys are great . . . (switch to Good/Bad questions).

In a situation like this, where they're already working with someone else, you really don't have anything and, because of that, you have nothing to lose. The goal of all of this is to see if the prospect will admit a problem. No problem? You can move on and call them back in 90 days or whatever your normal call rotation is.

Now let's talk about the super-negative prospect, the one you or your company burned a bridge with.

Super-negative prospect: How dare you call me. I hate your company! You asshats screwed me over last year!

Untrained salesperson 🐶: We didn't do it on purpose. It certainly wasn't *my* fault!

No BS Salesperson: Wow. I am so sorry. (If a prospect or client thinks you did something wrong, apologize. Own it. Tell them *you* are sorry. This is another pattern interrupt.) Sounds like we did something horrible. Tell me what happened.

Super-negative prospect: Well, you %&@$(&#%H, and that sucked!

No BS salesperson: I feel terrible about that. That's just awful. There's probably nothing we can do to make it up to you. Probably no way we'd ever be able to earn your trust again.

Super-negative prospect: I wouldn't say "nothing."

No BS Salesperson: What would you say?

In situations like this, the goal is to get someone to go from super negative to neutral. By taking the blame and falling on your sword, you allow your prospect to vent, which sometimes is all they need to do. This might let them see past the incident.

About 25 years ago, I went into a men's clothing store in town. I wanted to dress better, but, quite frankly, I didn't know how. When I went into the store, I was wearing a poor-fitting suit I'd had for a long time. I was looking at suits on the rack, and I heard one of the salesmen mocking me behind my back. I got really embarrassed and left the store in a huff. I was mortified and swore I'd never go back there.

Fifteen years later, I met another salesman from that store at a networking event. He, of course, was dressed to the nines and came across to me as a cocky asshole. (Much of this was my projection on him, of course). Some weeks later he called me, and

I told him I wasn't interested in buying clothes. He said he wasn't calling me to sell me clothes; he wanted my help learning to sell.

We had a good conversation, and he shared some real pain. Before we agreed to work together, I had to tell him. "I want you to know, I don't like you. If that's going to be a problem with us working together, let's not start." He laughed and said, "Look. I think you're an asshole yourself, but you know stuff I need to know. I don't need any more friends."

That guy has been one of my best clients for the last 10 years. We've even become friends. Good friends. And people tell me I'm dressing a lot better than I used to. And that started with a conversation about how we hated each other.

CHAPTER FOUR CHECKLIST

◆ Pick two or three questioning strategies, and put them to use.

◆ Start in a low-risk environment, like with "squirrel" prospects or with friends to see if you can get them to admit to a problem.

◆ Practice your ninja questions, but maybe start practicing with ninja phrases first: "Probably not the case with you . . ." or "This may be a dumb idea . . ." are good places to begin. After you get comfortable with the phrases, start using the pattern of Softening statement -> Negative statement-> "Let me ask you a question" -> Ask a question.

◆ ◆ ◆

CHAPTER FIVE

DISCOVER AND DISQUALIFY

L et's take a moment to recap what you've learned up to this point. With the first step, pre-call plan, you plan your sales call *before your meeting,* including what questioning strategies you want to use, what outcomes would be ideal, as opposed to *just okay,* where you could screw the call up and what your biggest fears are.

During step number two, you manage expectations with your prospect. Remember my awesome acronym: TADB, pronounced TAD-buh? When you meet with your prospect, you negotiate Time, Agenda, Decision and Biggest Fear to make sure that you're both on the same page. You set boundaries and rules to level the playing field. TADB helps you manage both your and your prospect's expectations for what will happen during the meeting and what decisions will be made at the end. No surprises.

The third step is to use the questioning strategies we discussed to solicit and understand your prospect's opinions about their situation. Do they admit having a problem they want to fix?

Once you start figuring out the problems that they're dealing with, it's time to tackle the fourth step of the No BS Sales System: Discover/Disqualify.

In this next step, it's time to see if you can **disqualify** your prospect. I know what you're thinking, *WTF, Walker? What do you mean see if I can DQ the prospect? She admitted she has a problem. It's go-time, right?* Not yet.

Not everyone with a problem deserves your proposal. Not everyone with a problem gets a demo. Not everyone with a problem is willing to fix it.

The No BS Sales System is meant to slow you down—to keep you from wasting time with people who aren't ready for you yet. Use the Discover/Disqualify step to learn:

1. If your prospect has a personal compelling reason to fix the problem (Pain).

2. If they are ready, willing and able to spend the right amount of money to make their pain go away (Budget).

3. If you understand their decision-making process and whether it allows you to keep your leverage throughout the sales process (Decision)?

No pain, no sale.
No budget, no sale.
No decision parameters, no sale.
No reason to waste their time.

PAIN: THE UNIVERSAL MOTIVATOR

If you've been in sales for even a minute, you know that *pain* is a buzzword tossed around by a lot of people. *Find your prospect's pain! To win their business, you have to find (and fix) their pain!*

They're right, of course. Uncovering your prospect's pain is critical—so important that I'm devoting this entire chapter to it. I'll teach you about using Budget and Decision to complete the discover-disqualify process in the next chapter.

Plenty of people will say you ought to find your prospect's pain, but few give advice on how to do that. I'm going to show you the actionable steps. These steps were inspired by a counseling approach called Motivational Interviewing, developed by a couple of clinical psychologists to help alcoholics and other addicts find their own genuine motivation for change and get a better sense of the likelihood of their success in a treatment program.

"The more you try to insert information and advice into others, the more they tend to back off and resist. This was the original insight that generated our search for a more satisfying and effective approach," one of the psychologists, Stephen Rollnick, wrote. "Put simply, this involves coming alongside the person and helping them to say why and how they might change for themselves."

Let's begin by discussing the pain-pleasure theory of human motivation. The assumption is that humans seek pleasure and avoid pain. Pain, it should come as no surprise, is a far more powerful motivator than pleasure.

In fact, studies show that there are five basic levels of human motivation. Here they are, ranked from lowest motivator to highest.

1. Interest, arousal, curiosity

2. Future pleasure

3. Current pleasure

4. Fear of future pain

5. Current pain

In the context of sales, when the motivation is "interest, arousal or curiosity"—lowest on the scale—price is usually the first consideration before a purchase. When the motivation is "current pain"—the highest—price almost doesn't matter. Or, to flip that equation, the more expensive (or disruptive or uncertain) making a change is, the higher your prospect's motivation needs to be to make that change.

I'll illustrate those five levels of motivation with five levels of stories.

Let's pretend that my wife and I have no children, but we are expecting a child soon. I'm wandering around the mall one day (unlikely, but, hey, it's just a story), and I end up in a toy store. I come across a satiny blanket quilted and sewn to look like a bear. It's called a Lovie. With a baby on the way, I'm **interested and curious**. *This is cute,* I think. *It reminds me of the blanket I dragged around as a toddler. I should buy it.* But when I turn the box over and look at the price tag, I see that it costs $80. *Holy shit! I'm not about to spend 80 bucks on a baby blanket. These people are nuts!*

To illustrate the second level of motivation, **future pleasure**, the situation is the same, except that our baby was just born. Wandering around the toy store, I spot the Lovie and pick up the box to check the price, thinking, *My son might like this in a couple of years. I wonder how much it is?* I flip the box and see that it costs $80 and think: *Maybe later. This is cool, but I have other priorities right now.*

In the scenario illustrating level three—**current pleasure**—my son is now two years old, and I'm in the toy store. I see the Lovie box and immediately check the tag. *Eighty bucks is kind of steep,* I think. But now that we're regular customers, I have a 20% off coupon. *Yeah, I can spend 64 bucks on that. My son will love it. This makes perfect sense.*

In the level-four scenario, **fear of future pain**, my son is now three and has his own Lovie. And like the name suggests, he loves it. He drags it around all day, sleeps with it at night. It is literally his security blanket. So, one day, I'm walking around the toy store and spot a Lovie that's exactly like the one he has. It now costs $85, but, boy, that would be a hell of an insurance policy. So, I buy it, take it home and put it in the closet as backup in case he loses the one he has. That feels like a no-brainer to me.

In scenario five, I never bought that second Lovie as a backup. My son is three years old, and we've just left the airport and are headed home from a family trip. We're all tired and cranky after a long day of airplane travel. All of a sudden, my boy starts to scream. He can't find his Lovie.

Oh, shit, I realize. *He left it on the airplane.* My wife and I exchange looks of horror. No way they'd let us back in the airport to get it. My son is inconsolable and screaming nonstop at the top of his lungs, so we rush straight to the toy store, even before going home.

I jump out of the car at the mall and run into the store as fast as I can, my wife following me with the crying baby.

"I need a Lovie," I tell the woman behind the sales counter.

"I'm sorry, I just sold the last one," she says. "That lady getting in her car over there bought it."

I bolt out the door thinking, I *need* that Lovie.

"Excuse me," I say, approaching the stranger with a sheepish smile, hoping not to scare her. "The sales lady said you bought the last Lovie. Is there any way you'd sell it to me? I'll give you $100."

"Well," she says, looking dubious. "I bought it for my grand-daughter, knowing she'll love it."

"I'll give you $200 for it."

She looks at me like I'm crazy but agrees to sell it to me for $200. I look in my wallet and find eight twenties. I'm $40 short. *Oh, shit.* My wife is standing behind me with my screaming son. She grabs her purse and pulls out $40 of next week's grocery money to make up the difference. Price is not an issue. We'll figure it out. We feel **current pain**.

When you're feeling pain *right this very moment*, your motivation is high.

Every single one of your prospects feels pain about something. The question is: Are you good enough to find out what it is? And, if so, can you fix it?

GOING BATTY

Years ago, after my wife and I bought a house, the contractor I had hired to do some work pulled me aside and said, "Hey, you've got bats in your attic."

Shit!

"How much would you charge to make them go away?" I asked. He quoted me a price of $900.

We were already spending a buttload to buy this house and fix it up. I didn't have an extra 900 bucks to spend getting rid of bats in the attic. It just wasn't a priority. Moving in and starting a family was. *They'll leave on their own*, I figured.

Three years go by. I'm in Maine for my annual fishing trip. My wife's at home, bathing our toddler son. "Look, mommy, a bird," he says, pointing from the tub into the hall. It's a bat.

I get home a few days later and hear all about it. That night, we're in bed asleep when I feel something touch my face. I figure it's some kind of a bug and, swatting it away, I make the kind of groggy bargain a sleep-deprived parent makes, silently telling the roach that, if it leaves me alone, I'll let it live.

Before I drift off to sleep, I hear a gentle but persistent scratching. *Deal's over*, I think. *You're dead.*

I turn on a flashlight so as not to wake up my wife and see a bat crawling along the baseboard toward the closet—the closet with a ladder that leads to the attic. That bat had just been on my face.

My wife has had a fear of bats since she was a child. I'm convinced she'd rather have a pack of wolves in our bedroom than a single bat. Trying to keep this problem to myself until I've solved it, I tiptoe downstairs and gather up a box, a broom and a glove. Not exactly MacGyver, but it's what I find to work with. Back upstairs, I slowly open the bedroom door; Sally is awake. She looks at me with my box, broom and glove, and says, "Walker, what the hell are you doing?"

"Look," I say, "Please work with me here. There's a bat in our room. It went into the closet."

She leaps up and starts a panicked dance on the mattress, bouncing like it's a trampoline.

"I'm going to catch it," I say. "Either help me or get out of the way."

She runs across the hall to be with our son.

I find the bat and palm it into the box. Then I find another bat.

The next morning, a Tuesday, I call my exterminator. "I have bats," I say, "and I have to get rid of them. If I don't, either my wife's going to burn the house down, or she's going to shoot me."

"Okay. I'll be there on Friday," he says.

"Friday? No, no, no, no, no."

I Google "bat removal" and call the first company on the list. A guy answers the phone, and I tell him that I have bats in my house and that I need him to help me.

"How do you know you have bats?" he asks. (Great Columbo question, right?)

"Well, one landed on my face."

He comes over. He's a big hairy guy, with an associate who looks like a rat. The two have been up all night chasing bats, he says. I show him the attic ladder in our bedroom closet. He climbs up and then climbs down real fast.

"Damn, I almost forgot to put on my gloves," he says. "I had a buddy who climbed a ladder, put his hand on the sill, a bat bit him, and he died."

He's standing there with his size 14 boot planted on my son's playmat, and he says, "You don't have kids, do you?"

"In fact, we do."

"Have you ever read those studies about the effects of bat guano on child development?" he asks.

"Uh, no," I stammer.

Then he climbs the ladder, opens the hatch and whistles. "Yeah, you've got a problem. Jeez, do you smell that?"

"Smell what?"

"You don't smell that bat piss? Is there something wrong with your nose?"

He climbs down and says, "Mr. McKay, I can fix this, but it's going to be expensive."

He goes to his truck and runs some numbers. "You're not going to like this, Mr. McKay," he says. "When were you hoping to have this done?"

"Today!"

"I was afraid you were going to say that. I can do it, but it will cost $8,500. I'll get rid of the bats. The attic will be cleaned out by tomorrow morning. And they won't be able to get back in."

What can I say? I write him a check.

Walking back to his truck, I ask him, "Do you know what I do for a living?"

"No," he says. "Are you a lawyer or something?"

"I teach people to sell—like you just sold me. How'd you learn to do that?"

"Do what?" he says.

Behold the power of current pain.

PROBLEM VS. PAIN

Some salespeople look for a problem and then tell their prospect that the features and benefits of their product or service will fix the prospect's problems. "What's wrong with that?" you might be asking. Here's what's wrong: How many problems do you have? Five? Ten? Me? I've got a million and probably more, but I only have the time, bandwidth, money and give-a-shit to focus on one or two—or *maybe* three—at any time. Your prospects are the same way. Just because something is a problem, or you can point it out as a problem, doesn't mean there's any urgency for them to address it, much less devote the necessary resources to fix it.

If your prospect's problem is causing them pain, however, that's different. *Pain is the personal compelling reason behind a problem that drives them to fix it* **now**.

The prospect must first admit a **problem**. After that, they need to share the **consequences** of that problem. The next step, where the pain actually resides, is in the **personal impact** of that problem.

A problem is when your truck breaks down, and you have to wait for the towing services and repairs. The *consequence* of the broken-down truck is that you can't get to work. The *personal impact* of not getting to work—the pain—is that your boss has already told you that if you miss one more day, he'll fire you, and you desperately need this job.

In another case, maybe your cash flow sucks. That's a problem. The *consequence* of crappy cash flow is that you can't pay your bills this month. The *personal impact* is that this is the third month in a row you've missed paying rent, and the landlord said if you can't pay the rent, he's going to kick you into the street. That's real pain. (Reminds me of one of my favorite George Thorogood songs!)

Pain is the emotional gap between where you are and where you want to be. Pain is personal and specific.

Often your prospect doesn't know they have pain, or they've misread what's causing it. I have a friend whose knee hurt like hell, and his doctor told him he needed knee-replacement surgery. So, he got a knee replacement. After the surgery and recovery, his new knee hurt like hell, too. After several more visits to different surgeons, he realized that it was never his knee that was the problem, but rather his hip. A problem in his hip radiated pain down to his knee. It was a misdiagnosis, because no one looked beyond the original symptoms. Like a surgeon, it's your job to make sure you understand what's *causing* pain—not just where the symptoms are presenting.

What's causing pain often needs to be teased out. First you need to discover if there is a problem. Remember, sometimes your prospect doesn't know what good looks like, and, therefore, they see no problems. That's where that questioning arsenal comes in. Those questioning strategies can help you help your prospect determine if they have a problem.

Once they admit they have one or more problems, then you need to figure out what the consequences of those problems are. After you've learned the consequences, then you find out how those consequences impact them personally. It's tempting to jump to the end—to tell your prospect what their personal impacts *must be*—but you risk missing the mark and losing your prospect. The magic happens when your prospect realizes *for themselves* the personal impacts that they hadn't been aware of before.

THE PAIN TEST

How do you determine if your prospect's problem is really pain? I use the Pain Test, a sequential list of questions that helps your prospect get to the source of their agony. The Pain Test is an essential part of the discover-disqualify process and one of the most important aspects of my system.

When you help your prospect identify the root cause of their pain by asking them the Pain Test questions, they'll see you as a trusted advisor, which will help you close business faster and at higher margins. These questions are meant to be asked one after the other until you get the information you need to make a decision to either move forward or not.

Here are the Pain Test questions, in order:

1. Can you tell me more about that?

2. Can you give me an example?

3. How long has this been happening, or how often does it happen?

4. What have you tried to do about it?

5. Did that work?

6. How much has this problem cost you? It can't be *that* much, right?

7. Is that a big deal?

8. What happens if you don't fix it?

9. What do you think you should do about it?

10. Are you open to outside ideas for how to fix it?

Let's talk about each of these questions individually, so you can see why they're important in our process of building trust and finding pain.

1. Can you tell me more about that?

Let's pretend you share a problem with someone you trust, and they say, "Wow, can you tell me more about that?" in a tone that is curious and sympathetic. How would that make you feel? Chances are you'd feel that person has an interest in you and your problem.

By asking your prospect to "tell you more," you're letting your prospect know you're listening and are interested in them. Your competition would have already spouted their solution, but you're approaching this differently.

Our brains can process thoughts at about 1,250 words per minute, yet even a fast talker can speak only between 100 and

125 words per minute. A thousand thoughts can be cruising through your head, but you can only speak about them a little bit at a time, and then they're gone. When someone answers a question, you get only nine or ten percent of what they're really thinking and feeling. The rest is gone. There's no way your prospect will feel understood if you don't continue to ask. By asking your prospect to expand, you give them the opportunity to slow down, process their thoughts thoroughly and give you as much detail as they can so you can more fully understand their situation as they explain it to you.

2. Can you give me an example?
While it's valuable to you, the salesperson, to hear their answers, it's even more important to your prospect to say them out loud. When people speak, a certain vibration of the jaw happens that makes them own any statement as "their truth." If they haven't said it, I want you to assume that it hasn't happened or that it isn't their truth yet. That's why you need to ask for examples—for both clarity and context.

Be careful not to accept a general answer. Gently ask, "Can you be more specific?" Or say, "Tell me the last time that happened." You want to give them space to think back on the specific time or times the problem occurred.

3. How long has this been happening, or how often does it happen?
Context matters here. Is the problem constant, or is it sporadic?

Adjust your question depending on what you've learned so far. If the problem is that their current vendor is terrible at communication, "How long has this been happening?" is better than "How often does this happen?" If it's that their equipment keeps breaking down, even after paying for expensive repairs, then "How often does this happen?" is a more relevant question.

Another thing to keep in mind: If this problem has happened only once or just recently, then maybe the prospect thinks it was just a flash in the pan and will go away soon. If it's been going on for 20 years, do you think they'll really believe you can fix the problem?

By asking these questions, remind yourself that, while you benefit from hearing their answers, it is the prospect that benefits the most in the long run. Because once they say something, it becomes their reality. You're helping them unspool the tangled thoughts in their heads.

4. What have you tried to do about it?
Now that the prospect has identified that there's a problem, has given you examples and told you how long or how often it happens, it's time to ask about consequences.

Among the first consequences would be how much time/effort/money/resources the prospect has spent to address the problem so far. Maybe they've tried 100 things, and nothing worked, or maybe they've not done anything because they didn't know what to do. Like before, it's good for you to hear their answers, but it's also important for the prospect to say it. When they say it, they own it.

The failed steps in the past are consequences that may have personal impacts on your prospect. By asking them to break down what they've already tried, you're allowing them to slow down and remember. All of this is valuable information to help your prospect put the problem into proper context. Often, when they're able to put into words what's happened and how they've tried to fix it, they can more clearly see the consequences of the problem.

And, equally important: By learning how they've tried to fix the problem, you avoid suggesting the same failed solution.

5. Did that work?

This might feel like a dumb question, but you'll be surprised with the answers you get. Sometimes they'll say, "Yep, it worked." And you can say, "Okay—it sounds like it's no longer a problem, then," at which point they can reconsider their answer. If they believe it did work, you can move on to another problem, but keep this one in the back of your mind for later. But if they tell you it didn't work—and it probably didn't—you want them to say *that* out loud.

I will often add a softening statement like, "I know this sounds like a dumb question, but did (any of) that work?" A common answer will be, "Of course, it didn't work. Why do you think I'm talking to you?"

With each step in the Pain Test, you're probing deeper and deeper into their emotions. As a result, around this point, your prospect might start to sound and look aggravated. Don't worry, they're not mad at you. They're mad at the problem. You didn't cause the problem, and you aren't part of the problem. The problem is theirs. They're just coming to grips with the consequences. Be calm, act empathetic and keep moving.

6. How much has this problem cost you?

Now it's time to quantify the consequences. *Cost* doesn't have to mean *money*. It can cost time, emotional energy and resources.

Money, though, can be a good place to start. You're helping them put a number on their problem. This is going to be very important when we get to the Budget step.

"It's been awful. I've had to let go of a bunch of good employees. I've spent $300,000 on stuff that didn't work. I haven't slept well in three months! God, I think it's probably cost me nearly $500,000 already if I consider the bad PR I got from having to fire people I couldn't afford to keep!"

You may be saying to yourself at this point, "I'm very uncomfortable right now. I don't like how uncomfortable this person is. It's really not my business how much this has cost her."

Let me quickly correct you. This *is literally* your business. You must hear these things firsthand, and your prospect must tell you so you can help them.

One thing to remember: Cost is relative. Don't make assumptions. Just because you believe half a million dollars is a lot of money, that sum may not mean much to someone else. To find out, slip in this bonus question after they tell you what it has cost them: "It can't be *that* much, right?" Yup, challenge it. If they exaggerated the number, you want to know that right now. Chances are the opposite has happened. Not every time, but many times, they'll respond to your challenge by saying, "Hell, it's probably more!"

7. Is that a big deal?

Seems like a ridiculous question. You've just watched them become agitated. They shared with you how much the problem has cost them in time, energy, emotion and money. Now we need to ask them if it's a big deal?

131

Yes, you do.

See, unless it comes out of their mouth, you can't count on it being their truth. You know what's funny? Clients have told me they're afraid the prospect will look at them like they're stupid and say, "Of course, it's a big deal. Are you an idiot?" If sounding stupid is your worry, say so: "I know this sounds like a stupid question, but is this a big deal?" Keep in mind as before, if their response seems grouchy or aggressive, they're aggravated by the problem and not you. You're simply helping them peel back the layers and determine for themselves if this is a big deal.

Because it's not always a big deal. I once talked to a guy who told me he had a problem that cost him more than $1 million the previous year. I was thinking, *Hell, yeah, I got this one!* Then, I asked him if the million-dollar problem was a big deal to him, and he said, "Nope, it's not in my P & L." Poof. No sale. Why? It was only a problem. Being *just a problem* is not enough. There were no personal impacts for him—no pain. How much time could I have wasted showing him how we could fix a problem he wasn't motivated to fix? A lot.

By the way, if you do have a situation like that—where your prospect identifies a problem and then identifies the consequences, but those problems and consequences don't impact the person you're talking to—is it over? Hell, no, it's not over. You can ask, "Well, who is this a big deal to?" The sooner you figure out you're talking to the wrong person, the better.

8. *What happens if you don't fix it?*

This is where you will learn their pain—the personal impacts of the consequences of the problem. Each question builds upon the previous one. With this question, learn their opinion about what will happen if they do nothing. You have to take them to this place in their head and heart so they can say out loud what will happen if they do nothing.

9. What do you think you should do about it?
I want to hear what they think, of course, before I offer my opinion. It's perfectly reasonable *and great* for them to say, "I don't know. That's why I'm talking to you." Sometimes they might tell you their thoughts and plans and give a few suggestions. Their plans may not make sense, but so what? Because your last question will be:

10. Are you open to outside ideas for how to fix it?
You must ask before you share your ideas with your prospect. Don't give advice without first asking permission. Why? Let me tell you a story.

A while ago, I had insomnia. It was terrible. I walked into one of my sales-training classes one morning, and there to greet me was one of my students, Jamie. She was one of my favorites. Jamie was from a little country town. She had been her town's beauty queen and was also a weightlifter. She had big hair and big muscles. One of the things I loved about Jamie was that she'd been engaged for nine years. Instead of an engagement ring, her fiancé gave her a nickel-plated 45, because, she said, nothing shows love like a Colt 45.

When I walked through the door, Jamie looked at me and, in her wonderful country accent, said, "You look like shit! A real mess!"

"Thanks," I said. "I've got insomnia."

She immediately responded, "You should eat more fish!"

All of a sudden, bombs went off in my head. I thought to myself, *What an idiot.* But I didn't say it out loud because she might have shot me.

I composed myself and taught the class. Afterwards, I thought to myself, *Why did I react that way? She was just trying to be helpful, even if it was a little weird. What was it that got under my skin?* As I thought about it, I realized it was because she hadn't earned the right to help me solve the problem yet.

I wondered how it would have been if she said to me, "Insomnia? Tell me more about that."

I might have said, "Well, I fall dead asleep every night around 10 o'clock. At 1:30 a.m., I wake up like a shotgun has gone off. My heart is racing. My brain's going a million miles an hour."

"Can you give me a specific example?" she might have said.

"Yes, that exact scenario happened last night. I woke up at 1:30, as usual, and was pacing and out of sorts until around 4:30 in the morning, when I fell dead asleep again until 5:00, when my son woke up screaming. At that point, nobody in the house slept anymore."

"Well, how long has it been going on?"

"My son's six months old. Um, it's been going on about six months," I would have said.

"What have you tried to do about it?"

"Let's see, I've used earplugs. I've gone to the doctor. I changed my exercise routine. I gave up booze for a time. I gave up chocolate."

"Wow! Did any of that stuff work?"

"Look at me. Hell, no, it didn't work!"

"What do you suppose that has cost you?"

"Well, I can't think at work. It's probably cost me $100,000 in lost deals. I don't know what a damn divorce costs, but that would be a lot. I'm not exactly shaping up to be the ideal dad. How do you put a value on that?"

After a couple more questions, if she'd then asked if I'd be open to outside advice, I'd be primed to hear what she had to say. Hell, I'd welcome it.

Let's pretend she used a third-party story like, "Well, I have a friend with a similar problem who did a lot of reading about insomnia. She learned that omega-3 fatty acids can help your brain calm down. She ate salmon every night for a week and every other day for the next few weeks. After a couple weeks, she started sleeping through the night—at least until her own child woke her up in the morning."

Essentially, it would have been the same advice—eat more fish—but had she taken me through the Pain Test, she would have earned the right to give me that solution. At that point, I probably would have canceled class, driven to the grocery store and filled my car with salmon to eat on the way home!

Don't give anybody a reason to think you're an idiot because you gave the solution before you completely understood their pain and earned the right to do so.

Where can you use this? Everywhere. Practice the Pain Test questions in your everyday life. When your friend says, "My shoulder hurts," or your boss says, "I hate our office space," say, "Tell me more about that" and "Can you give me an example?" Take them through the Pain Test, and you'll be amazed at the conversations that will open up between you and people you've known for years but have never had a deep conversation with.

A warning: Don't ever do the Pain Test on your spouse, because, well, you're probably the source of their pain. You don't need to remind them of that any more than you already do!

CHAPTER FIVE CHECKLIST

♦ Memorize the 10 questions in the Pain Test—in order. The order matters because you're slowly digging deeper and earning the right to do so as you ask each one.

♦ Practice the Pain Test in low-risk situations, like when a friend or co-worker shares a problem. Notice how easy it is to do when you have nothing to sell to solve the problem. Friendly reminder: Don't do this with your spouse. Don't remind them that you're the pain.

❖ ❖ ❖

CHAPTER SIX

BUDGET AND DECISION

hate doing yardwork.

In South Carolina in summer, it's oppressively humid and hot. I don't like being outside pushing a lawnmower and trimming bushes when it's that miserable. So, I quit doing it. Problem was, I didn't have a plan for what to do next about the yard, so nothing happened. It didn't take long for the yard to look completely overgrown and messy. My wife, worried about what the neighbors would say if we let it keep growing, said that I either had to clean up the yard myself or get someone else to do it. So, I called a neighborhood teenager who does yardwork and told him I wanted his help. I showed him what I wanted done, and I asked him if he could help me and how much he would charge.

Then he asked me a question that surprised me. He said, "Mr. McKay, what are you expecting to spend to get your yard cleaned up like you talked about?"

"Well, Johnny, I'm not really sure how much it will cost," I said.

"No, not how much it would cost, but what were you expecting to spend?"

"I don't know, 75, 100 bucks," I said, picking figures off the top of my head, hoping I was right.

"Oh, no, Mr. McKay. It's going to cost more than that. Last week I did the Johnsons' yard, which is about the same size as yours, and it cost $200." (Nice third-party story, by the way.)

"Holy shit! Two hundred bucks?" I said.

"You could definitely do it cheaper yourself. You have a lawnmower, right?"

Whether he knew it or not, this kid was pulling a nice ninja move on me.

I started weighing my options. I was already pouring sweat and swatting the gnats buzzing around my head just standing in the yard talking to him. No way I want to do this myself. I could probably call around and find somebody else, which would take time and most likely wouldn't be any cheaper. Or, I could just hire Johnny to do it now.

"It's a deal," I said.

As I walked away, I thought, *Damn, that was good.* This kid asked me about my budget—how much money I was ready, willing and able to spend for him to do the yardwork. And the best part of it was that he was able to put it into context, because I'd already told him how much I hate doing yardwork. He helped me realize that, while $200 felt like a lot of money, giving it to him was a whole lot less painful than me pushing the lawnmower and trimming the bushes on a hot summer day or wasting time calling around to get the same answer from someone else.

If I could get salespeople to ask the simple question—"Do you have a budget for this?"—it would make all the difference in the world. Ideally, they would 1) learn how much their prospects are ready, willing and able to spend and 2) give them the context of how much it will cost to fix their pain.

But asking about budget is hard for a lot of people. Really hard.

THE BUDGET TEST

We ask about the budget after we've found out our prospect's pain. Why? Because pain puts the budget into perspective. Here's an example:

There were these engineers who were in charge of a nuclear plant. It was kind of a boring job most of the time. But today was different. At 9:00 a.m., all the alarms went off, the warning lights flashed on and all the gauges pushed into the red zone. The engineers panicked because they didn't know what to do. There was a sign on the wall with a phone number and a message: "Call in case of an emergency!"

So, they called. A woman answered and calmly asked, "What's going on?"

The engineer on the line shouted that all hell had broken loose at the plant and that, if they couldn't fix it fast, the fallout could impact millions of people. The woman said, "I can help you, but it's going to be expensive." "We don't care! This could be horrible!" She told him to put $500,000 in cash in a briefcase and hand it to her as soon as she arrived.

"Okay," he said. "But please hurry!"

She arrived 20 minutes later and asked for the briefcase. She opened it, counted the money and then handcuffed the case to her wrist. She walked over to the back of the control room, opened a cabinet and flipped a switch inside. Immediately, things went back to normal. The engineers were baffled. "We paid you half a million dollars to flip one switch?" they said. The woman said, "No, you paid me half a million dollars because I knew which switch to flip."

Money and value are relative. Each is measured in the mind of the beholder at the time of the discussion. Remember: Current pain is the highest motivator.

There are two reasons people struggle to ask prospects about budget. One is conceptual—their beliefs about money. Maybe they were taught as a child not to talk about money, or something about their current financial situation makes it hard to talk about money. Or maybe they struggle to understand what "a lot of money" means to other people.

The other is tactical. They just don't know the words to use to talk about budget.

Let's talk about both.

First, conceptual. Money is a difficult subject for many people. Your idea of "a lot of money" versus "not so much money" is completely subjective. It can stem from how you were raised, how you're living at the moment or how you perceive those living around you.

My Dad had no trouble talking about money. He would get into someone's car or walk into their house and say, "Nice. How much did you pay for it?" His belief was that people loved to tell him how much they paid for stuff. My mother, on the other hand, would cringe when he asked that. Money was a taboo topic. She told me to never talk about money. She was quick to tell me that "Money doesn't grow on trees," and, "Don't waste your pennies. They grow into dollars."

Because of these mixed messages, money was always a complex subject for me. It's amazing how a green piece of paper with a dead guy's face on it causes so many salespeople to falter.

Some of us create a self-fulfilling negative-feedback loop about value: It starts with belief and then circles through behavior, results and feelings. If you think your product or service is too expensive—or *you'd* never spend that amount of money on it—you hold the **belief** that it is too expensive. As a result, your **behavior** (or lack thereof) is not to ask your prospect about their budget, hoping it won't be an issue. When it is an issue, it's often at the end of your sales process after you've spent a bunch of time sharing how you'd fix the problem. The **result** of this is that when they push back on price—either in a move like "The Flinch," (see below) or they truly don't have the budget—you'll have no choice but to cut your price or lose the sale. This will reinforce your original **feeling** that "our price is too high," thus beginning the cycle again.

DON'T FALL FOR THE FLINCH

Have you ever witnessed a move prospects make that's known as "The Flinch"? You know what I'm talking about. You share your price, and the prospect acts shocked and says, "*What?* That's ridiculous! That's way too much money."

If you have a poor money concept, you'll fold like an old T-shirt when that happens. Chances are you'll drop your price as low as you can go to avoid more (fake) conflict. And when you drop your price, do you realize what your prospect just learned? That you tried to screw them out of however much money you discounted. They'll demand a discount every time you try to sell them something. And why wouldn't they?

On the other hand, have you ever been in the position where you have no room in your price to cut, and when your prospect pulls "The Flinch," you just say, "I'm sorry. That's as low as I can go"? You know what happens most of the time, right? They'll say with a smile, "Well, I had to ask." See, it's a game for them. It costs nothing to tell you your price is too high. But it can cost you and your company a fortune over time. I don't have specific stats on this, but if I had to guess, crappy salespeople around the world give up at least a billion dollars every single day in margin because they fall for "The Flinch." If I were a buyer's coach, I'd be fully on-board with my clients using The Flinch every time they're quoted a price on anything. Why not? It works like magic against salespeople with money weakness. And there are a lot of you out there!

When you're selling business-to-business, most of the people you're dealing with are spending money that's a line item on their budget. Most of the time it's not even *their* money. They're going to spend it somewhere. It might as well be with you. If your prospect has pain, they can almost always find the money to fix it. They'll just pull it from some other line item or from some other project that's not so important right now. If they can't find the money, it's probably a good sign that you didn't find their real pain.

I'm fairly certain you've been asked to cut your price before. You quote a price of $1,000, and your prospect responds with, "I'll give you $900." If you agree to $900, you just admitted you were trying to jam them. The lesson your prospect will get is: "She tried to rip me off!!! If I hadn't said anything, she would have stuck it to me." Every time after, they'll demand a discount because "they caught you" last time.

If you're in a situation where you choose to lower your price, make sure you get something in return. For example, before you agree to cut your price from $1,000 to $900, ask, "Let's pretend I'm able to cut $100. If I do that, what happens next?" Or, "I can give you the lower price, but you'll have to sign a longer contract." Or even, "I can do this less expensively. Which part of this do you want to cut out?" Another response could be, "Okay, how well does this need to work?"

Do you have any customers/clients/prospects who have to negotiate everything—everything is about them getting something extra? Like the whole thing is a game that they must win? I call those folks "Players." One thing I know about Players is that they love another Player. If you're dealing with a Player, when they ask about price and you know they're going to want to negotiate, say: "We can do this one of two ways, and either one is okay with me. The first way, I'll give you a higher price so we can negotiate down to the real price. The second way, I'll just give you the real price and that's that. We'll end up in the same place either way. You pick."

They'll always say, "Give me the real price."

Now you respond with, "Okay, I'm happy to give you the real price. My biggest fear is that you're asking for the real price, but you're going to want to negotiate from there. If that's going to happen, let's start with the higher price instead."

So, what can you do if you have conceptual issues about money that are holding you back?

1. Work to shift your mindset: Reframe your idea of asking about budget from prying into someone else's affairs to discovering how you can best help them with the budget they have.

2. Role play: Use sales meetings or one-on-one coaching time to role play, asking about budget in a low-pressure situation. The more you practice, the easier it will be to do it in real time.

3. Offer multiple options: It can be a good practice to offer a good/better/best scenario to your prospect with prices that are commensurate with each.

4. Be completely transparent: Say, "I hate talking about money; it makes me very uncomfortable, but I know we need to do it. I gotta ask, do you have a budget for this?" Just put your cards on the table and see what happens.

Let's assume that you've taken care of your conceptual issues. You understand that what you think your product is worth has absolutely nothing to do with what your prospect might think.

Whether you think it's too expensive or not expensive enough, it's all a matter of context for your prospect.

That brings us to the tactical—the words you should use. I call this series of questions the "Budget Test."

The first part is super easy. Ask, "Do you have a budget for this?" That's not too scary, is it?

There are three possible answers to "Do you have a budget?"

1. Yes

2. No

3. Yes, but . . .

Let's take the easy one first. When you ask somebody "Do you have a budget?" and they say "Yes," you say, "Great, how much is it?" and shut up. Wait for them to answer.

What if they answer "No" when you ask if they have a budget? It might mean they don't have any money. It could mean there's no line item in their budget. Or it might mean they have no idea how much it would cost. At this point, you don't know which one it is. If you ask if they have a budget, and they say "No," I want you to take them literally and ask: "So, how would we proceed if you don't have a budget?" At that point, they'll explain what they meant by "No." If they have no money, you want to know that ASAP.

"Yes, but . . ." is slightly more complicated. They will probably follow with one of three responses:

1. "Yes, but I can't tell you because of corporate policy."

2. "Yes, but I don't trust you." (It may not be those specific words, but that's the essence.)

3. "Yes, but I don't know how much it is (or how much this should cost)."

If the answer is "Yes, but I can't tell you because of corporate policy," they're probably being honest. Many companies have policies, often used to keep salespeople in the dark. You still need some sense of how much they're planning to spend to fix a problem. You don't want to assume they're budgeting $100,000 when, in reality, it's more like $10,000.

One way to get around the strict policy is by using a few phrases to soften things up. "Do you mind sharing with me, off the record, round numbers for what you were hoping to spend?"

By the way, what do "off the record" and "round numbers" mean? How is that different from "How much is it?" It's not different, but it will give your prospect some space to share a number if they are so inclined.

If you are still getting nothing, you can follow up with, "Maybe you can give me a range? If you're thinking $10,000, and I'm thinking you're thinking $100,000, or vice versa, I'm afraid I'd be wasting your time." It gives them a way to give you a clue. If you get shut down here, too, you might decide to make the business decision to walk away. How will you be able to help someone if you don't know how much money they'd be ready, willing and able to spend? If you decide to stay in the mix, however, when you present your solution, offer a good/better/best option with different price levels, covering all of your bases.

One caveat: Be sure you're willing to deliver on any of the three and price it accordingly.

If the answer is some version of "Yes, but I don't trust you," you've still got some work to do. Maybe they say (or are thinking), "You'll just make it that number," or "You want to take away my ability to negotiate." Usually, their body language is a tell. They get tense, look away, or appear uncomfortable or defensive. If you're getting that feedback either from their words or their body language, calmly respond: "That makes sense. I completely understand. Look, my price doesn't change based on the number you give me. We can do something for a low price, and we can do something for a higher price, and the solutions would be different. I'm just trying to make sure I offer you the best solution based on your budget. If you could give me an idea—maybe a range—I can show you what an option that matches that might look like. Can you help me with that?"

This also works with the third scenario: "Yes, but I don't know how much it is (or how much this should cost)." Once again, reassure them that your price doesn't necessarily change with their budget, but the solutions might. You just need to know *generally* what they're prepared to spend.

Below are three ways you can help your prospect get more comfortable giving you a budget number, so that you'll know which direction you'll need to go.

HISTORICAL PRECEDENCE

If someone who's bought it before says, "I don't know how much this should cost," you can tell them how much they spent the last time and work from there. "Is that still going to be okay this time around?" Usually, if they've spent this much money before for the same thing, it makes it easy to agree again.

THIRD-PARTY STORIES

Next is our old friend, the third-party story. Instead of talking about what they've done before, you might share what other people in the same situation have done, like Jimmy the lawn mower. Remember, budget is not where you tell somebody how much it costs. It's where you figure out how much they're ready, willing and able to spend.

When using a third-party story, you can say, "Others in a similar situation typically spend somewhere between X and Y." Give them a range and follow up with, "Does that range work for you?" Make the range wide and use the number that you think it should be as your **low** number. For example, if you're guessing this is a $1,000 solution, give the range of "between $1,000 and $1,500." That way, if you need some room to go up, you've got it, but if you don't, your prospect won't feel like they got jammed.

BRACKETS

You may have caught on by now that I'm big on ranges. Instead of specific numbers, give ranges or brackets that the prospect would be comfortable with. You can make it as ridiculous as "We might charge you anywhere from $100 to $1,000,000. For

$100, you might get advice over lunch. For $1,000,000, we could train your entire sales team in Hawaii." You're showing them that you need their help in narrowing things down.

If an absurd range won't work—for instance, if you're selling a product that's already fairly well known in the market—then try a more specific range, maybe a 15% or 20% difference between X and Y. If you think something will cost $100, say it could be between $100 and $120, depending on when they need it and any upgrades or extras they want. Give a tight enough range and say, "Does that range work for you?"

Typically, salespeople with money weakness will mention the cheapest prices to attract the prospect. The problem is, if you say something will cost $80 to $100, and it ends up costing $110, you'll have your prospects raising their eyebrows. "That guy skinned me. He charged me full price plus!" Be real. Be upfront. It gives you room in case there's a problem or you have to deliver it overnight.

Products and services can be commoditized, but your prospect's pain cannot. This is why it's so important to ask them about their budget. Get a number so you know what you're dealing with.

Using the Budget Test, you can gauge the services you can provide for the money they are willing to spend.

And if they don't pass the Budget Test—if their number doesn't match what you need to have or if they don't have any money—you're done. And that's completely okay. Say something like this: "You know, it sounds like I'm talking to you at the wrong time. We can get back together when something has changed."

BUDGET TEST FLOW CHART

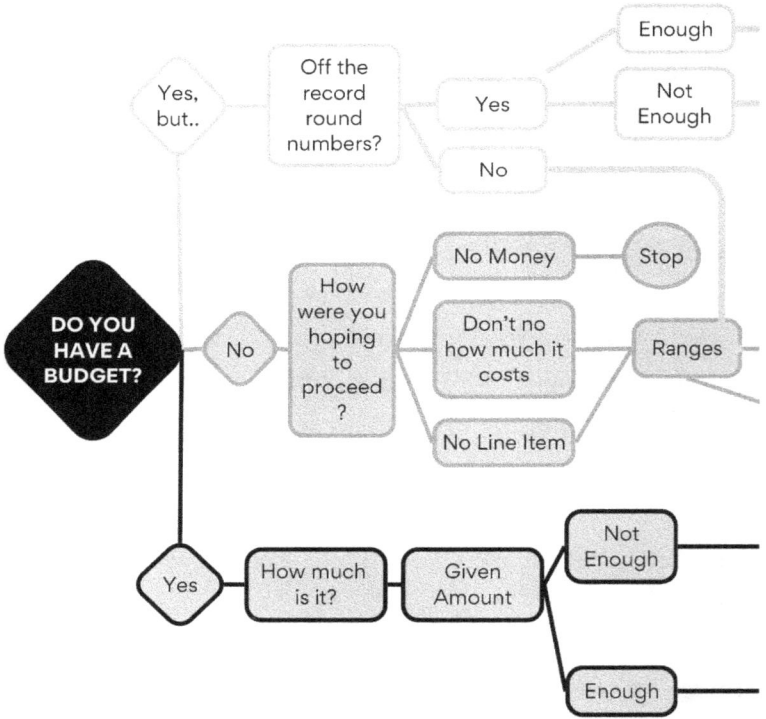

Enough

Off the record round numbers?

Yes, but..

Yes

Not Enough

No

No Money — Stop

How were you hoping to proceed?

Don't no how much it costs

Ranges

DO YOU HAVE A BUDGET?

No

No Line Item

Yes

How much is it?

Given Amount

Not Enough

Enough

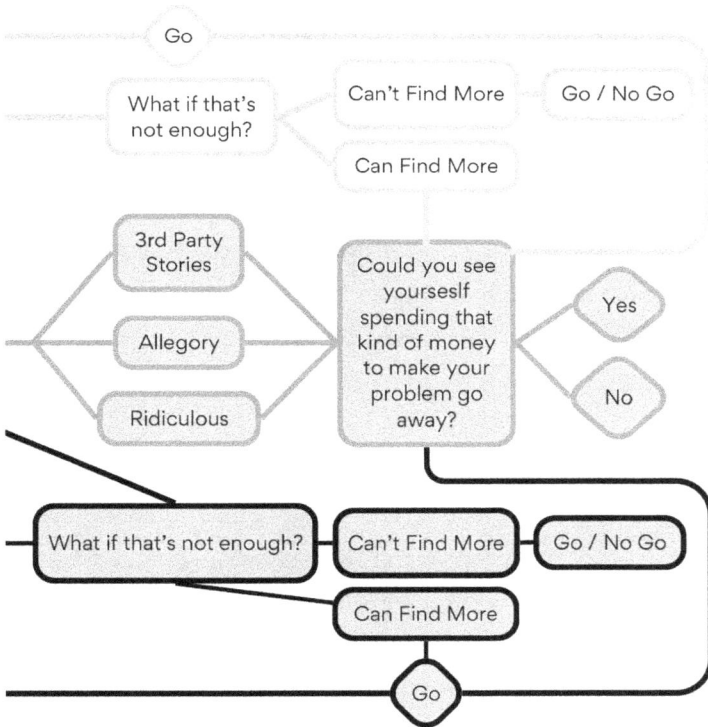

On the other hand, if they do pass the Budget Test, then you can start figuring out the range of products and services you can provide. You can give them a match that suits their needs.

While I've talked about budget as being money, there's more to it than that. Depending on what you sell, you might also need to know if they could devote the time and/or resources to fix the problem. Yes, my training is expensive, but it also takes time out of the field to master. Depending on several factors, someone could spend an hour or two a week in training with me for a long time. It gets less intense over time (again, based on many factors), but if they can't carve out time, it doesn't matter how much money they have. "Resources" is code for *people*. Sometimes your solution may require some number of your prospect's people to change focus and work on something new. Think software implementation or switching to a different benefits plan.

THE DECISION TEST

You've learned in this chapter and the one before how to identify your prospect's pain and figure out how much money, time and resources they're ready, willing and able to spend to make their pain go away. Now we need to learn about their decision-making process. This tends to be easier than identifying pain and budget, but it's just as important.

The old-school sales guy approaches it like this: "Are you the decision-maker?"

You might be thinking, *Yeah, what's wrong with that? It's straight to the point. No BS.*

It's a lame question because it doesn't tell you what you really need to know.

By working through the Decision Test questions, you'll get the level of specificity you need.

There are five questions you'll need to get answers to before you've nailed the Decision Test: When? Why? Who? What? and Who else?

Start with:

1. *When?*

"When are you hoping to have that fixed?" or "When are you planning to make this decision?"

What's their time frame? If they're not planning to decide for, say, two years, I can't think of a good reason to give away all of your information now. Can you? The world will be different two years from now. Hell, the world changes every day these days. If you give someone your proposal a long time before they're planning to make a decision or even to devote the resources to fix it, not only will you have no leverage at decision time, but I can guarantee your information will have been shopped to your competitors. Or they'll have figured out how to do it without you. Remember, in the discover-disqualify phase, we are not disqualifying our prospects forever. What you're trying to decide is whether they qualify to get your information now. Be skeptical. Make them prove to you that now is the right time.

2. *Why?*

"Why do you need the problem fixed then?" or "Why make the decision then?"

You might be able to uncover additional pain here. They might say that they need to have it fixed because it's impeding some key process of the business or that there is some impending event that they have to get ahead of. If there's no good reason why they have to make a decision soon, there's a good chance they won't. If they say they have no real time frame, you need to go back and find more pain. Your prospect will see right through any attempt you make to "create urgency" for them to buy. Stop trying to create urgency. Uncover it instead.

3. *Who?*

"Who else needs to be a part of this decision-making process?"

I know what you're thinking: "Nice one, Walker. You just slid in an assumptive question!" Yes, I did. You have to admit that it's a far better question than, "Are you the decision-maker?" First of all, "Are you the decision-maker?" may be offensive to the person you're talking to, but that's not the main reason for not asking it. The main reason is that it's not that good of a question. Maybe they are the decision-maker. Maybe they're the owner or the CEO. But what if they want to bring the CFO or HR director into the conversation? Or their business partner? You want to know "who else" so you can suggest all of those people be there when you share your solution, and not be surprised when they say, "Well, of course, I need to talk to my business partner before I sign this."

4. *What?*

"What is it you need to see or hear from me to be able to make a decision?"

You want to give someone only the information he needs to make a decision. If all someone needs to know is what color your solution is and the price, don't talk about what shape it is. We believe that other people are either like us or should be like us. If we need hundreds of pages of data to make a decision, we assume everyone else does, too. If you think something is particularly cool or exciting about your solution, you're going to be tempted to share all of that with your prospect. *What's wrong with that?* you're probably asking. I have a story to illustrate what's wrong.

A man and his wife were expecting a child in a couple of months and wanted a car that was safe, reliable and had enough room to carry around all the stuff that comes with babies. They went to a Honda dealer and were looking in the windows of a Honda Pilot. His wife had owned and loved Hondas in the past and was hoping the Pilot would fit the bill for her next car. The salesperson came out, introduced herself, unlocked the door and began to talk about the car.

"The Pilot is a great choice. It has lots of features like a leather interior, a big back-up camera and a great stereo." They looked at each other and nodded in approval. They took the car out for a drive and decided this was the car for them. The salesperson was excited to make one last sale on the last day of the month. This would get her a bonus. As the couple walked into the dealership to sign the paperwork to buy the Pilot, the salesperson said, "This car has a special sealant on the carpet that makes it resistant to spills and stains. It's made by Scotchgard." The husband looked at his wife in horror. He whispered, "We can't buy this car. I've been reading about all the chemicals in Scotchgard and how toxic they are to humans! What if our baby licks it and gets sick, or worse?!"

Sale blown.

I am not a need-tons-of-data-to-make-a-decision person. If someone can't sell me in one page, another 30 pages won't help. I've learned, however, that others may need more info than I do. While it pains me to create longer, more-detailed proposals, I'll do it if that info makes my prospect more comfortable making a decision. Like a lot of other things in sales, we need to give the prospect what they need (to a certain point), not what *we* want or what *we think* they need. I once had a prospect tell me he needed ten references—five people who would say good things and five who weren't satisfied with my service, before he would buy. I quickly ended the conversation.

5. *Who else?*

"Who else, besides me, are you talking to about solving this problem?"

Have you ever assumed that you were the only one your prospect was talking to and then later found out that you were one of three? That's a kick in the ass, isn't it? It's not that you wouldn't do as good of a job if you knew you didn't have competition, but maybe you'd button some things up a little more or even offer a couple of different options (good, better, best, for example).

If you've got competitors or even if you don't, you want to know as soon as possible. Right now. Ask, don't guess.

When and only when you know the following—when your prospect is going to make a decision, why that date matters, who besides them needs to be part of the process, what all of them would need to see or hear from you, and who, if anyone, might be the competition—should you move toward closing.

If you do have competitors, you want to present last. Yes, last. If you're last, you can ask for a "yes or no" decision at the end of your presentation. You can also ask questions like, "When the others asked you about _____, what did you tell them?" Or "What impressed you most about the other vendors?" And then, once that's fully explained to you, "What's one thing they left out that you wish they hadn't?" "Which of those two is your first-choice pick now?" "What was it about that one that made it your first choice?" "What would you hope to hear from us that would make you comfortable that we'd be your first choice?"

Are you with me now that the old-school question "Are you the decision maker?" has been shown to be not only lame but also not helpful.

You've now learned the three parts of discover and disqualify: pain, budget and decision. In the next chapter, I'll cover closing a deal. One cool thing about the No BS Sales System: You close *before* you present. Yes, that's right. You'll close before you present.

How is that possible? you may be asking. Move on to the next chapter to find out.

CHAPTER SIX CHECKLIST

- If you struggle to ask prospects about budget, identify what's holding you back. Is it conceptual, tactical or both?

- Review the Budget Test, and role-play the different scenarios so you can respond accordingly when you're on a sales call.

- Memorize and practice using the five questions in the Decision Test.

❖ ❖ ❖

CHAPTER SEVEN

THE CLOSE

You've gone through the Pain Test with your prospect, and you now have a clear picture of their main problems, the consequences of those problems and the personal impacts of those consequences. Using the Budget Test, you now understand the money, time and resources that they can spend to fix the pain. And you now understand their process for making decisions. Now it's time to talk about the close.

In the No BS Sales System, you close *before* you present. This is one of the biggest differentiators between the No BS Sales System and other sales methodologies. I know what you're thinking: "That's bullshit." But hold on, and I'll show you how. The lesson begins with the no-pressure close.

FOLLOW THE 5 Cs OF CLOSING

My best clients tell me they love the no-pressure close in the No BS Sales System. These five steps: Condense, Confirm, Commitment, Closing Agreement, and reConfirm take the pressure off you and the prospect. It confirms that what you're looking for is a decision, but not necessarily a yes—just like you both agreed on in the opening agreement at the beginning of your call. It's respectful to all parties because it gives both sides agency. The prospect isn't committed to buy, only to make a decision. The seller, you, isn't obligated to give the presentation if the timing still isn't right. And, like the rest of the No BS Sales System, it allows everyone involved to be real with each other.

1. CONDENSE

Let's start with the first one, which is to condense what you heard from the prospect as they shared their pain, budget and decision. It might sound like:

"So, you said you're having trouble with cash flow, you're concerned about your employees and there was a problem with your shipping partner. Those things are costing you about a million bucks a year, and if you don't fix them, it could be the end of the company, which would be horrible for you and your family. You said you could spend around 20% of that, about $200k, to fix those problems. You mentioned that this needed to be fixed as soon as possible and that you can make the decision, but you want input from your CFO, so he needs to be at the meeting as well. Finally, you said you need to see exactly what it is we're going to do to fix these problems, including the timing and the cost."

It's simply taking what they told you in the pain, budget and decision tests and combining them into a small capsule to let the prospect know that you were listening and that their opinions matter to you. This technique of repeating back to someone what they themselves said is very powerful. It can be used throughout the sales process to make sure you understand and to reinforce the impact of your prospect's own words and ideas.

2. CONFIRM

The second, confirm, is pretty easy. It can sound as simple as, "What did I miss?"

Here, they'll either explain further—sharing more pain—or they'll simply agree and verify everything you've condensed so far. Either way, it's a win.

3. COMMITMENT

The third step is commitment. If the prospect is not committed to fixing the pain they've been discussing with you, when do you need to know that bit of information? (I want to know right now!!) This is just one more thing to clarify before you share your information. I worked with a plumbing company some time ago, and one of the guys called me, laughing, as he left the sales call. "This lady had a shower head that kept dripping even after two plumbers had been out there before," he told me. "It wasn't going to be an easy fix. I asked her how committed she was to making it stop, and she said she wasn't. I was, like, 'What?' and asked her what she was going to do. She said, 'I'm going to sell this house. It's a piece of crap!'"

The script here is pretty easy, too. "How committed are you to fixing this problem in the near future? Not necessarily with me, but with someone?" What you're looking for is an emphatic, "I am very committed to fixing this." Use your gut here, but if you sense any hesitancy, follow up with, "Sounds like there are a few things you need to fix first before you can address this." No commitment, no sale.

4. CLOSING AGREEMENT

The fourth step is a Closing Agreement. Remember in "Chapter Two: The Necessary Preparations," when we went over the importance of an opening agreement—negotiating upfront how the sales call should go? Agreement on the time, the agenda, the decision that would be made at the end of the sale? We are going back to our friend, reciprocity—If I do this for you, will you do this for me?—to make sure we're all still on the same page. Now, you're restating the agreement to make a decision at the end of the meeting. Here's what a closing agreement might sound like:

"All right, I'm going to show you what I would suggest you do to make this problem go away, and I'll answer any questions you have. If I'm okay doing that, are you still okay telling me whether or not you want to move forward?" Please note: This is not, "If I show you a way, would you buy today?" as so many cheesy salespeople ask in order to corner their prospect. This is, "Are you still okay making a 'yes or no' decision to the step we've agreed upon?"

A warning, though. After going through the Pain, Budget and Decision Tests, you may have to modify what you're agreeing to decide. You may have opened up a larger can of worms. It may be a bigger problem than they expected, or the decision about whether or not to move forward may involve more people and money than you or your prospect initially expected. This is why a closing agreement can be essential for making sure you're still getting to a decision with your prospect.

Make sure you are both very clear about what you're agreeing to make a decision about. Is it yes or no to signing a contract? Yes or no to bringing the CFO in? Or even yes or no to scheduling another meeting? Whatever it is, make sure both parties clearly understand the mutual agreement about what's going to happen next.

AGREE ON AN ACTION STEP

Be clear with your prospect about what happens next if he chooses your solution. Depending on how your conversation has already gone, one of these things might be appropriate:

◆ Sign a deal/get money.

◆ Get another meeting.

◆ Agree that the prospect will endorse you to a boss or other decision-maker.

◆ Take a smaller, paid step. (Remember the Monkey's Fist story from Chapter Two?)

---

5. RECONFIRM

The last is to confirm again. You might say, "All right, let's do this: Anything less than you thinking doing _____ is a great idea, let's call it a 'No.'" I've even put it this way: "Look, if you're not thinking 'Hell, yes, let's do this,' let's call it a 'Hell, no.' Is that okay?" If this sounds scary for you to say in real time, I get it. The reality is, anything less than them being excited about you making their pain go away means you've got a problem.

I met with the CEO of a bank last year. We went through the whole process, and we got down to the close. I started with the first of the five steps: *condense*. I said, "So, what I heard you say was that you're concerned because your younger bankers aren't especially good at bringing in new business. They're pretty good at making friends, but they're not so good at closing deals. And when they do bring in business, they have to discount the rates to get it.

"You said this is costing you four, maybe five hundred grand a year in lost margin and fees. While 'deals not won' don't have to be reported to investors, it does impact your earnings. The board of directors and Wall Street analysts are expecting big growth, and, if you can't produce, it's going to impact not only the value of your options but also your relationship with the board. Your job may be in jeopardy. You said that you are able to make this decision and that you can pull money out of the marketing budget—around $100,000—if we figured out how to fix the problem."

I moved to *confirm*. "What did I miss?"

"Nothing. I think you got it," he said.

"Okay. Tell me something," I said, moving to *commitment*. "How committed are you to fixing this problem?"

"I'm really committed."

"So, there's nothing more important that you need to take care of first?"

"Nope," he said. "This is my number-one priority."

"Great. Let's do this," I continued, now with the *closing agreement*. "I'll show you what I think will fix the problem. If I'm okay doing that and answering all of your questions, will you be okay telling me whether you want to move forward—meaning signing the contract and giving me a check, like we talked about?"

He said, "Sure."

It was time to *reconfirm*. "Anything less than that, let's call it a 'No,'" I said. "Is that okay with you?" **Notice I'm pushing for a "No."** What I don't want is some "think it over" bullshit. Like we've talked about before, I want you to consider "I want to think it over" and all of its derivatives ("I'll need to check with my partner, who's in Europe with no phone," "I need to sleep on this," "I gotta get board approval," "Call me in two weeks") as a long "No." Might as well hear it now.

"Perfect," he said.

The deal was closed. We'd come to an agreement that: 1) I understood his opinions about the situation he and his bank were in, 2) he was committed to fix it and 3) that I was going to show him what I thought would be a good solution. When I was done and had answered all of his questions, he would be comfortable telling me whether or not he wanted to move forward with my plan. If he didn't want to hire me, no big deal—we'd still be friends. If he did want my help, he knew that the next step would be to sign my contract and get me a check.

MAKE THE SALE

After the close, you finally get to show the prospect how you're going to fix their problem. Here, I'll teach you how to get your prospects to close the sale themselves and how to avoid losing a sale you've already made.

The first step is to repeat their pains back to them and ask them to pick the one they want to address first.

I recently met with the president of a medium-sized commercial insurance brokerage. We already had a closing agreement to decide whether or not she would hire me for training and coaching. Everything was set up, and I said, "Okay, you told me about three main issues: You think your hiring process is broken, you've got new brokers taking too long to become profitable and most of the new business you've gotten is because you were lower priced than the competition, which is hurting your margins and increasing client churn. Which one of those do you want me to talk about first?"

She said, "I gotta figure out the hiring thing."

"Great," I said. "Let's talk about hiring. First of all, we'll help you implement a hiring process that we'll customize specifically for your situation. Our best clients tell us having a repeatable and iterative process helped them weed out some of the weaker candidates. We'll help you with everything from determining who your ideal hire would be (background, skill level, work ethic, temperament) to how to write the ad and the best places to put it. We also recommend using a specific third-party assessment to determine each candidate's sales skill level and their mindsets for sales."

I walked her through a few more ways I would help with hiring and said, "Any questions about the interview process?"

"No. That sounds great!"

"Excellent," I said. "What do you want me to talk about next?"

"Getting these new producers to be profitable," she said.

"Great. Here's what we'd do to fix that: Remember that assessment I mentioned for hiring? We have a similar one we use for existing members of the sales team. Each producer will take it during the first week we're on-board.

"Simultaneously, we'll create a behavior/accountability plan for newbies and existing producers who're not yet profitable. Each week, we'll get them to report on how many calls they've made, how many connections they've had, how many meetings they've set and how many 'No's' they've gotten. Once we get them on the behavior plan, we'll start training skills and mindsets based on their assessment results. I need you to be aware that we may cause some turnover. Some people will be mad when they're held accountable for doing the hard work in sales. Will you be okay if we lose those people who don't want to be held accountable?"

"Hell, yes, I'll be okay," she said. "It would be great if they'd fire themselves."

"Don't expect miracles in the first 90 days," I told her. "You said this problem has been going on for a long time, and it's probably going to take some time to fix it."

When I was done, I asked, "Any questions about the plan to help the newbies become profitable?"

"Yeah," she said. "I'm curious about having the reps count their 'No's.' What do you mean by that?"

"Well, you know sales reps can't control who buys, but they can control what they themselves do," I responded.

"Sure," she said.

"We want every interaction to end with either a 'Yes' to move forward or a 'No' to stop. We want the brokers to be comfortable preparing their prospects to give them a 'Yes' or 'No' at every step along the way. I see 'No's' and 'Yes's' as having equal value. If I get a 'No' at the first meeting, that's a whole lot better than getting one in the fifth or sixth meeting. So, if our brokers are asking for a meeting and getting a 'No,' that's progress. I want the 'No' to be counted as it should be, as a win."

"Okay," she said. "I get it!"

I confirmed that she agreed with me, that she thought the steps I outlined would make the problem go away.

"Any other questions about our plan to get your brokers to be profitable sooner?"

"Nope, I'm good," she said.

"How comfortable are you that that plan will solve the problem?" I asked.

"I think that's exactly what we need."

THE 10 SCALE

My guess is you've cooked chicken on the grill before. Chicken is tricky because, if you undercook it, not only is it gross to eat, but you could also get really sick from chickenosis or whatever it's called. The other problem is, if you cook it too long, it's like trying to eat shoe leather. One way to make sure you get it just right is to use a thermometer. When the center temperature is between 165 and 170 degrees, the flavor and texture will be perfect, and it's time to pull it off the grill.

Knowing when to finish presenting and close is a lot like knowing when to pull your chicken off the grill.

If you try to close too soon, it's messy, and the results of not making the sale might make you sick to your stomach. If you go on too long, talking about the things your prospect doesn't care about, you can burn your prospect out, bore them to tears or, even worse, bring up stuff that they hadn't thought of and screw up your sale.

The 10 Scale is a simple tool you can use to judge how committed your prospect is to buy from you. Even better, when it's the right fit, your prospect will close themselves.

So, after you've shown your solution to two pain points, answered any questions they have and gotten positive feedback from your prospect that they believe your first two solutions will work, pull out your closing tool, the 10 Scale. It's the simplest and most accurate way I've ever seen to learn where your prospect is on their buying journey and, when the time is right, to allow them to close themselves with no pressure from you.

Here's how you can bring it up: "I don't want to waste your time, and I'm really not good at reading minds. Can you tell me where you stand, say, on a scale of 1 to 10—where 1 is *you wish you'd never met me,* and 10 is *you wish I'd shut the hell up so you could sign a contract like we talked about*?

I love the extreme examples of "wish you'd never met me" and "wish I'd shut the hell up" because that's what a real human might say. It's humble, yet right to the point.

You want a number. It might sound cheesy, but it's a great way to quantify how they're currently thinking about buying from you. First of all, if they respond with 5 or below, recognize that something has gone wrong. You've just shared your solutions for their top-two highest priority pains, and they give you a score of 5 or less? You've missed something. If they're at 5 or less now, it's not time to try to convince them to change their minds. It's time to pack up and move on. Apologize for wasting their time. That might sound something like this: "Wow, sounds like I've wasted your time, I'm so sorry. I'll close your file and let you move on with the rest of your day."

It's a good time to remember that your prospect's belief about your willingness to walk away is your ultimate leverage. You're not playing games. If you're like me, though, you'll want to know what happened, what you missed. In the No BS Sales System, we don't guess; we ask.

This is a perfect place to ask a Columbo question. After you stand up, grab your stuff, head for the door, turn around and, like a good detective, say: "Do you mind if I ask you a question? (pause) What did I miss? Usually when someone has problems like that, they're begging for my help, but I'm not hearing that from you." It's amazing what you can learn when you ask this question. Chances are you'll find the truth you weren't able to uncover before. Sometimes it can be the best place to restart your sales call.

I did this with a commercial property and casualty insurance guy a couple of years ago. He wasn't making enough money. His dad owned the agency, and he was afraid he was letting his old man down. He wanted to take over the agency one day, but, at this rate, there was no way that was going to happen. I laid out a plan to get him to where he wanted to be. He said he was a 5.

I apologized for wasting his time and got up to walk out. I grabbed the doorknob, turned around dramatically and asked him gently, "What did I miss?" He gave me a bunch of excuses about why he couldn't do the work I was going to ask him to do. I listened until he took a breath. I interrupted him and gently asked, "Have you lost your damn mind? You've shared all of this stuff with me about how you have to fix the problem, but now I show you the way—and you're a 5?"

He turned red-faced and began to reconsider. I sat down and pushed back hard. "It can't be that important to you. You can just go get another job. No reason to stick around here, right?" He ended up convincing me that he was committed to fixing the problem; he was just scared. He was single and had never committed to much in his life. Reminded me of myself many years ago. He just needed to be called on the carpet. Three years later, he was the number-two producer in the company, right behind his dad. Three years after that, he bought the company and has since added five more producers. While he gives me credit for turning him around, he did the hard work. All I did was challenge his bullshit. He did the rest.

If their answer is 6 or 7, that's progress. I like to challenge their number, no matter what it is. I did that with another prospect, a sales manager for a software company. "You chose 6? That's higher than I thought you'd be. Why are you even a 6?" I let her talk. I let her explain. Once she stopped, I returned to presenting.

"Okay, it makes sense that you're a 6. Which issue do you want to talk about now?"

"How do we keep them from discounting," she asked.

"Let's talk about discounting," I said. "This usually happens because the producer is caught in what we call 'the commodity trap.' That means the prospect can't differentiate between them and the competition. Everyone says they're different, but in the same ways. You know: *We've got better service, better people and better quality.* Just like everyone else. The only way for your people to differentiate themselves is in the way they act, not just what they say. We teach a simple sales process that's unlike anything your prospects have seen or experienced before."

"If it's anything like what you've done here with me, I can definitely see that it's different," she said.

I then followed up with, "Do you have any questions?"

"Nope."

"What else do you want to know?"

"When are the trainings?"

"That sounds important. Tell me why you ask." (Reverse, right?)

"Fixing these problems is super important. I want everyone to be able to attend."

"Okay. Typically, for the first 12 weeks, we meet as a group once a week for an hour. This is so we can drill the fundamentals. After that, we meet every other week for an hour to do a deeper dive and reinforce the process and how it works in your company. My assistant will work with whomever you designate to find the right time for these meetings. Any questions about that?"

"Nope."

"Do you think that pace of training will work?"

"Yes."

I had gone over two more pains. Now it was time to check in again with the 10 Scale.

"Tell me again on a scale of 1 to 10 where you stand with my proposals."

If she had remained stuck on 6 or 7, I would have kept presenting and providing more details. If her number had dropped below that, it would have been time to call it "over." If her answer was 8 or 9, I would have asked, "What's one thing you need to see or hear from me to make it a 10?"

In this case, she said "10."

"That's higher than I thought you'd be. Why are you a 10?" I asked. After that, it was simple: "What do you want me to do next?"

You're probably jumping out of your chair asking, "What about price, Walker? When did she ask about the price? When did you tell her?" Great question. Throughout the process, I held back on revealing my price, and I recommend you do the same. Price is your ace in the hole.

If someone says, "I want to talk about price first," say, "That's great. I'm happy to talk to you about price, but do you mind if we look more closely at the problems? Because if you don't trust me to fix them, price doesn't matter. I promise I won't waste your time."

What matters most is whether they trust you to fix their problems. Delay talking about price for as long as you can.

Sometimes, you can't delay any longer. Before you give a price—and this is critical, no matter when it happens in your process—I want you to say, "I'm happy to talk to you about the price [notice the softening statement]. Before I do, though, let's pretend I give you the number, and you're comfortable with it. What do you see happening next?"

Why do I frame it that way? Because if they say, "Well, what are you going to do about this and this and this?" then hold back your price and say, "Let's talk about those things first." Don't die the death of a thousand cuts. If there's going to be a problem, learn about it right now.

Before you quote a price at the end, say, "Look, if I'm okay giving you the price, are you okay telling me whether or not you'll move forward? And if so, that you'll sign a contract or purchase order or write me a check? If you don't, no big deal. We'll call it a 'No.' Is that going to be okay?" Get your last closing agreement. Make sure that, before you give something, you get something in return.

You give your price, and then you say, "Okay, help me understand. Back to my dumb old 10 Scale again. Where are we?" At this point, what you hope they're going to say is "10," and your no-pressure close is: "Great. What would you like for me to do next?" It's not, "What do you want to do next?" but "What would you like for me to do next?"

Of course, some people can be hardheaded and never give anything above a 9. You can simply treat that as a 10 and do your no-pressure close to make the sale.

Use the 10 Scale. It's a powerful tool for identifying the right time to bring the sales call to a tidy ending. Let your prospect tell you when the right time is to get a commitment, and move forward.

When your prospect effectively "closes themselves," they've signified they have very high trust in you. You've just shown them the plan to move forward and away from their pain. They've moved from prospect to client.

MAKING THE SALE: SIX SIMPLE STEPS

You've reached a closing agreement. Now you get to show the prospect how you're going to fix their problem.

♦ Repeat their list of pains, and ask them to prioritize.

- Give a solution to their #1 pain/answer questions/confirm it's the right solution.

- Ask which pain they want to discuss next.

- Show solution to #2 pain/answer questions/confirm it's the right solution.

- Check in with the 10 Scale.

- If they're below a 10 here, go back to presenting, and repeat the process.

1-5 — Close the file, apologize for wasting their time; Ask **"What did I miss?"**	**6-7** — **"What would you like me to talk about next?"**
8-9 — **"What would you need to see or hear from me to be a 10?"**	**8-9** — **"What do you want me to do now?"**

LOCK THE SALE

Have you ever made a sale, gotten a contract and a check, only for the prospect to call a day later saying, "Wait! We've changed our minds. Something has come up. We've put a stop payment on the check and need you to tear up the contract!"

It's happened to me more than a couple of times in my career, and it sucks. I never wanted that to happen again. So, I created the last step of the No BS Sales System, called "Lock the Sale," to keep a sale from blowing up after it's already been made.

Great sales is all about managing expectations. Even when a prospect becomes a client, we need to keep letting them know what the future holds.

There are three common reasons sales blow up even after you've closed. One is buyer's remorse, when someone regrets the decision they've made. This can be spurred by others in the organization pushing back when they learn that a change is going to happen. The second is when the competitor calls the buyer crying and whining to get their business back, offering to cut the price and fix all the wrongs they've committed that caused them to lose the business in the first place. And the third is when there's a problem in your fulfillment stage, and something didn't work like they hoped it would.

The secret is dealing with all these things up front—before you leave the room—because doing so makes your job a whole lot easier.

Buyer's remorse can come in many flavors. Sometimes it's just someone waking up in the middle of the night panicked, saying, "Oh shit! I just spent a ton of money on that! That was stupid!"

Other times, it happens when someone announces, "We're going to start using another software that we're super excited about," and the people who are used to the old software panic and

say, "Whaat? We're not gonna change! We like the old way!!!!!!"
And the boss panics and cancels. If that's going to happen, when
do you want to know? Me? I want to know *now*!

So, if something like this has happened more than once,
you want to make sure you've warned your (now) client that it's
going to happen to them. AFTER they've signed the contract,
after money has changed hands, then you have to tell them, or,
even better, ask them: "When you wake up in the middle of
the night and panic because you just spent this much money on
new podcast equipment, what are you going to say to yourself
to calm down and fall asleep again?"

Let them work it out in their head in front of you, not after
they've already panicked. In the second example, we use another
assumptive question: "When your people freak out because you're
asking them to change the way they work every day, how will
you handle that?"

Bring up the worst-case scenario. Ask them what they're going
to do. If nothing like that happens, no big deal—nothing is lost.
If it does, then, at least they're prepared and you've taken a big
step to show them you've been there before and helped them
get through it.

The next thing that can screw up a sale after you've made it is
when your competitor finds out they got fired and begs to stay.
A wealth-management firm once asked me to help them hire a
new producer. We did a long search with specific criteria. We
interviewed a bunch of people and ended up finding this bad-ass
financial planner, whom we all thought would be a perfect fit.
She was great. She grew her book of business every single year
and rarely lost a client.

We met with her and learned that her pain was that she didn't like her current boss or the office environment. She was looking for a change. So, we made her an offer, even promising her a corner office with a killer view. She accepted the offer. That was a Thursday afternoon, and she planned to tell her boss the next morning she was leaving and starting with the new firm on Monday.

The next day, in preparation for her arrival, the firm ordered her furniture and her laptop. But around 11:00 a.m., after not hearing from her, I started getting worried. Noon came and went. At 2:00 p.m., I called her.

"I'm so sorry," she said. "I can't take the job."

"What do you mean?" I asked. I was shocked.

"When I told my boss I'd leave, he cried," she said. "He offered me a corner office and a raise. I feel so bad about backing out, but I'm going to stay here."

I thought, *Shit, what have I done? I've wasted my client's time. Of course, that was going to happen.* A few weeks later, we found a different candidate who also fit the bill. After he accepted the job and signed the agreements with us, I made sure we warned him of what was going to happen next.

"We are so glad to have you on-board. All of those things that we promised you would happen are going to happen. Here's something else that's going to happen: Your boss is going to freak out and beg you to stay. What will you say to him when he does that and offers you more money or the ability to work more from home?"

He said, "I've been asking for those things for three years. If it takes me quitting for him to see those things as being important enough to fix, that's not the relationship with a boss I'm looking for. I'll tell him it's too late—that I didn't quit just to negotiate a better deal with him."

The same approach works with a prospect who's about to fire an incumbent and give the business to you. Remember, people make decisions emotionally and then justify them intellectually. When the (former) incumbent calls and begs your new client to come back, you want to make sure they're prepared for that call. After you make the sale, you can say, "The guy you've been working with for the past five years: What do you think he's going to say when he finds out you're firing him?"

Pause, and let them answer the question. They may say something like: "Oh, he's going to be pissed. And he'll probably beg me to give him another chance."

You'll respond with a question, of course: "How will you handle it when he does that?"

And you can also ask: "Let's pretend he offers to cut his price or fix the service problem; how will you respond to that?"

Because if there's going to be a problem and the prospect might waver, you want to know that *right now*. A client who is prepared for the tough conversation is more likely to remain in their intellectual, adult state and stand up to the begging loser you just unseated.

The last thing we need to prepare our new clients for is a messy onboarding. Probably not the case with you, but some people sell stuff that takes a bit of effort to get set up or is complicated and takes some users a while to get used to.

I have a client who sells heavy equipment. After a sale, he dreaded the calls that sometimes came. Somebody would buy a giant bulldozer or some other complicated piece of machinery, and they'd turn it over to their operator onsite. There is always a break-in period where some things need to be worked out. Sometimes the technician from the shop needs to adjust something. Sometimes it's just a different setup than what the operator is used to. Either way, it causes confusion and panic.

So, I said, "Let's deal with this up front."

He now tells his new customers, these people who now hold him at the highest trust level: "Look, this machine has got like 4,000 moving parts and 17 different fluids. We have a 500-point checklist to make sure that everything is just right, but sometimes we miss stuff. Here's what I want you to do. I want you to take this out of here assuming everything's fine. But if in the next three or four weeks something's weird—a seal blows, one of the gauges goes off, or things aren't working exactly as you hoped—pick up the phone, call Nick in our service shop, and he'll send somebody out there immediately to see what's wrong, and we'll get it fixed. If you can't get Nick, or it's not fixed satisfactorily, pick up the phone and call me, and I'll call Nick and make sure it gets done."

Manage your customer's expectations. Prepare them for what might happen next. Your job to manage expectations is never over. It's even more important with your customers and your clients.

CHAPTER SEVEN CHECKLIST

In this chapter, you've learned how to share your solution and keep your leverage.

◆ Memorize and practice using the five C's for closing: condense, confirm, commitment, closing agreement and reconfirm. These steps remove the pressure on your prospect to tell you "Yes."

◆ Grow comfortable with using the 10 Scale as a tool to help you gauge how likely it is your prospect will hire you.

◆ Keep prospects from backing out of deals in three critical ways. Lock the Sale by: eliminating buyer's remorse, neutralizing the competition and pre-warning about possible implementation problems.

◆ ◆ ◆

AFTERWORD

YOUR NEW SUPERPOWER

Congratulations! You're almost done! It says something good about you that you've invested the time and mental bandwidth to learn a better way to sell. Now take the extra step and put what you've learned to use immediately. I'm going to recap a few things to remind you how to take the BS out of your sales.

You've learned how to avoid the prospect's trap and to adopt the four new mindsets you'll need to sell using the No BS Sales System:

* You're not the right fit for everyone.

* You have equal business stature with everyone.

* Ask, don't tell.

* Be the guide, not the hero.

You've learned how to prepare for your sales calls, and how to manage everyone's expectations. You have picked up key questioning strategies to help you build trust with your prospect and to get to the truth much more quickly. You have learned how to understand your prospect's situation to see if they have any concerns or problems—and how to help them make their pain go away.

You have also learned that, if your prospect has no pain, or that pain isn't a priority for your prospect to fix, or if there is no budget, or if their decision-making process doesn't make sense for you, then you can disqualify them and save you both a bunch of time.

You have learned how to close before you present and how to present without giving away all of your leverage.

Finally, you learned how to lock the sale to make sure you don't lose a sale you've already made.

By following the No BS Sales System—your system—you will close high-margin deals faster than you ever imagined, disqualify those prospects much faster who were never going to buy from you and make a lot more money. And you will be able to do all this without sounding, acting or feeling like a cheesy salesperson.

These new skills are like a superpower. Use them wisely.

As I said in this book's Foreword, however, deep down, making more money is not really what the No BS Sales System is all about.

Many of my clients tell me that their biggest takeaways aren't even about making more sales (even though that happened). They tell me they've learned how to have better conversations, to have more empathy and to keep from getting emotionally involved in things they can't control. And they're genuinely helping people solve problems and end pain.

I couldn't agree more.

Last year, I got a call out of the blue from one of my son's high-school classmates, a guy named Ryan, who was a rising college junior.

"Mr. McKay," he said, "I made cold calls from school to get a sales job this summer. I don't know what I'm doing, but I want to learn how to do it right. I was wondering if you'd be willing to help me?"

He'd gotten a job selling building-maintenance contracts to property-management companies. He was to do this by cold-calling strangers.

"I thought I would start selling this summer and get some practice," he said. "I know there's more to it than just pushing numbers on the phone and telling people how great our service is. I've watched your stuff on LinkedIn. Will you spend a few minutes on the phone giving me advice?"

I'd met Ryan before, but I had never had a real conversation with him. I'd always pictured him as kind of shy, and, truthfully, I didn't think much more about him than that. And now I was thinking, *Holy shit. This college kid cold-called and landed a summer job in sales.* He was selling one of the hardest things there is to sell—building-maintenance contracts. (It's not exactly selling ice to Eskimos, but it's not a simple sale.) *And he had the guts to cold-call me to ask for help?* You know how many college kids have called me and asked for sales advice? So far, only one.

"Hell, yeah, I'll help you," I said. "Let's meet for lunch."

At lunch, he explained that he wanted to run his own company. That he wasn't afraid of taking risks or working hard. That he wanted to forge his own path and that he knew that learning how to sell was crucial to his success. After we got to know each other a little bit, I asked him to walk me through his cold-call approach. No surprise: He sounded like a lot of salespeople. He talked fast, spat out facts and numbers and made promises, all in a desperate attempt to convince the prospect to buy—or at least to stay on the phone. Having received no training, he was using the old sales methodology, which he'd picked up by osmosis and, most likely, by observing the other salespeople at the company.

I explained the basics about the prospect's trap and taught Ryan how to flip things around by asking questions and not assuming everybody was a prospect. I urged him to be honest and transparent in order to gain equal footing with his prospects, to be a guide who helps the right people at the right time find the right path. Essentially, I walked him through the first steps of my sales training. Of course, I didn't charge him. He was young, ambitious, hungry to learn and open to outside ideas. Sounds funny, but I wish I'd had someone guide me like that when I was young and stupid. I probably wouldn't have been ready for the advice, unfortunately.

Ryan, on the other hand, was open to my suggestions and grateful for the advice—so grateful, in fact, that he convinced his boss, the sales manager, to contact me. Ryan's boss called and said Ryan told him he needed to meet me, but he sounded skeptical. His phone call swept me back to the first time I met Matt, the sales trainer. Was this guy going to meet me and try to smoke me out as a fraud, like I intended to do with Matt? Would he then have an epiphany about how he'd been approaching sales all wrong, how he'd been making excuses for his failures, how he was ready to bring change to his organization?

Nah. That's not what happened. He made it clear on the phone that they didn't need any help, but he wanted to meet me for lunch since he'd heard so much about me from Ryan.

"Certainly my team could be better at sales, but they're pretty good," he said, explaining that his salespeople didn't take "No" for an answer and would get aggressive on pricing when they needed to. He said that "every prospect we talk to gets a quote," and he was happy with their numbers. He was a super-nice guy. He wasn't arrogant or rude.

Did I think I could make a major difference in their sales results? Oh, hell, yeah. Without a doubt. I'd already trained one of his competitors to be the most expensive option and still beat this guy's company almost every time they competed. Did I bring that up? Nope. They weren't ready for me yet. Honestly, after talking to him, the thought of training and coaching him and his team made me feel tired. I had four more sales calls with new deer prospects in the following ten days and felt no pressure to even turn that visit into a sales call.

Ryan and I met three or four times that summer and had a couple of phone conversations. Turns out he sold three contracts, which is pretty damn good for a beginner, much less a rising junior in college who probably didn't really understand what a building-maintenance contract was. He said that the coaching I'd given him gave him confidence to take "No" for an answer, to walk away from deals he didn't think he could win and to keep reaching out to prospects, even when he didn't feel like it.

High on my bucket list is creating a program that uses the basics from my No BS Sales System to help other young adults like Ryan learn to be more direct, honest and transparent in their dealings with other people, no matter what their professional path. I'd love to help them eliminate excuses in their lives and communicate better. Help them build more trust, solve more problems for people and feel good about their work and themselves. In short, help them cut out the BS that seems to be so prevalent these days.

Part of that work is choosing not to waste time on people who are full of BS. And there are plenty of them. Which brings me full circle back to the title of this book: *Some Will. Some Won't. So What. Who's Next?*

There are plenty of great prospects out there. Go use the skills you've acquired by reading this book to see if they trust you enough to give you money to make their pain go away.

Ask yourself: Who's next?

❖ ❖ ❖

ABOUT THE AUTHOR

Walker McKay is the Founder and Principal of McKay Consulting Group LLC, and creator of the No BS Sales System™.

Walker believes that sales is the art of telling the truth and being transparent and the science of getting your prospect to do the same. He says "no" is his second favorite word and he hears it all the time.

He has been calling, networking and asking for referrals for over 35 years and training high producing salespeople for over 20. He's worked with hundreds of B2B sales teams to quickly disqualify deals that aren't the right fit, to close the right ones faster than anyone ever expected and to get better margins than any of their competitors.

He is a lifelong salesperson, coach and the creator of the No BS Sales School, where he trains his clients to use his proven and customizable sales process to exceed sales targets, grow revenue, and gain the respect they deserve.

Walker has been married to his wife Sally for 25 years and they have two sons, Walker III and Mitchell. He is the host of the No BS Sales School podcast found wherever you get your podcasts. You can also follow Walker on Facebook, LinkedIn and Twitter.

Walker would like to thank his friend and editor, Logan Ward, and the talented team at 1106 Design for helping make this book a reality.

Drop him a note at walker@walkermckay.com.